". . . SO GALLANTLY STREAMING"

". . . SO GALLANTLY STREAMING"

The Story of Old Glory;
The History and Proper Use of
Our Flag from 1776
to the Present

Compiled and Edited by
M. R. Bennett

DRAKE PUBLISHERS INC.   NEW YORK

Published in 1974 by
Drake Publishers Inc.
381 Park Avenue South
New York, New York 10016

© Snibbe Publications, Inc., 1971

Library of Congress Cataloging in Publication Data
Main entry under title:

So gallantly streaming.

   1. Flags—United States—History.
JC346.S6   929.9'0973   73–18120
ISBN 0-87749-604-8

Printed in the United States of America

Contents

The Origin of Our Flag	1
The Evolution of the Flag	3
When the Flag was First Flown in Battle	8
The Flag and the U.S. Army	9
Our Navy and the Flag	11
Old Glory and the U.S. Marines	14
The U.S. Coast Guard and the Flag	16
The Star-Spangled Banner	17
The Man Who Established the Flag	20
Dates of Admission of States	22
U.S. Flag Foundation	23
The Father of Flag Day	24
The Origin of Loyalty Day	26
Flag Plaza Foundation	26
The Pledge of Allegiance	27
The American's Creed	28
Names Given to Our Flag	29
Famous Songs About the Flag	31
Famous Paintings of the Flag	33
The American Flag by Francis R. Drake	35
A Toast to the Flag by John Jay Daly	37
Flag of Our Fathers by John Jay Daly	38
Famous Stories About the Flag	39
The Makers of the Flag by F. K. Lane	40
The Day I Belonged to the Flag by Dwight D. Eisenhower	42
Quotes by Famous Americans	43
Remember Me?	52
What the Flag Means to Me	54
What the Pledge of Allegiance Means to New Citizens	56

Contents

Unusual Places the Flag Was Carried	58
The Flag at the North Pole	61
The Flag Around the World Under Water	62
The U.S.S. Francis Scott Key	63
The Flag Flies on the Moon	64
The Flag on Postage Stamps	66
When First Flown Over a School	70
Flag Saluting in Schools	72
Famous Large Flags	74
The Largest Flag in the World	76
Flag Makers	77
Flag Terms and Phrases	78
The Flag Research Center	79
How Well Do You Know Old Glory?	80
Flag Etiquette:	
When the Flag Should Be Displayed	81
Special Days to Fly the Flag	82
National Flag Week	84
Where the Flag Flies Day and Night	85
Hats Off! The Flag is Passing By	88
Our Flag Flies Above All the Rest	89
Respect When Flown With Other Flags	90
Unfurl Her Standards in the Air	91
In Churches and Auditoriums	92
During Public Affairs	93
At Unveilings and Burial Services	94
Proper Respect for Our Flag	95
Our Flag is Not A Decoration	96
When Flown at Half-Staff	97
Misuse of the Flag	98
Use of New and Superseded Flags	100
Opinion of the U.S. Supreme Court	101
Bibliography	103

The Origin of Our Flag

Most people in the United States think that the Stars and Stripes were ordered by General George Washington, that Betsy Ross sewed the first flag and that the Revolutionary forces used this flag from the day the Declaration of Independence was signed.

The story of the Stars and Stripes is the story of the nation itself; the evolution of the flag is symbolic of the evolution of our free institutions and its development into the great nation it is today.

In the early days of the Republic, when the Thirteen Original States were still British Colonies, the banners borne by the Revolutionary forces were as varied as the races that made up the liberty-loving colonists.

The local flags and colonial devices displayed in battle on land and sea during the first months of the American Revolution carried the various grievances that the individual states had against the Mother Country.

The first public reference to the flag was published on March 10, 1774. A Boston newspaper, the Massachusetts Spy, ran this poem to the flag.

"A ray of bright glory now beams from afar,

The Origin of Our Flag

Blest dawn of an empire to rise:
The American Ensign now sparkles a star,
Which shall shortly flame wide through the skies."

On June 15, 1775, when General Washington had been appointed commander-in-chief of the Continental forces for the defense of American Liberty, the Continental Congress was still corresponding with King George to present their grievances.

In the fall of 1775, the revolting colonies chose a flag that reflected their feeling of unity with the Mother Country, but also expressed their demand to obtain justice and liberty.

In Taunton, Mass., a flag was unfurled in 1774 which carried the British Jack in the canton, and was combined with a solid red with the words, "Liberty and Union," printed on it.

The famous Rattlesnake flag carried by the Minutemen in 1775 showed thirteen red and white stripes with a rattlesnake emblazoned across it, and the warning words "Don't Tread on Me."

In 1775 the banner that flew over Fort Moultrie displayed a crescent on a blue field with the word "Liberty" printed in white. When this flag was shot down by enemy muskets, a brave sergeant named Jasper nailed it back to the staff at the risk of his life.

The Pine Tree Flag which flew over the troops at Bunker Hill in 1775 displayed the pine tree symbol of the Massachusetts Bay Colony. It was a white flag, with top and bottom stripe of blue, and it showed a green pine tree with the words, "Liberty Tree—An Appeal to God."

The first flag or ensign to represent the colonies at sea was raised by John Paul Jones from the deck of the ship Alfred, on Dec. 3, 1775. A month later, George Washington displayed this same design and named it the Grand Union Flag. This was on Jan. 2nd, 1776. It had thirteen alternate red and white

The Evolution of the Flag

BRITISH ENSIGN

TAUNTON

BUNKER HILL

NEWBURY

WASHINGTON'S CRUISERS

LIBERTY TREE

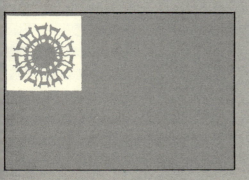
LINKED HANDS

CONNECTICUT

The Evolution of the Flag

RHODE ISLAND

MOULTRIE

CULPEPPER

GADSDEN

NAVY JACK

CONTINENTAL

GRAND UNION

BENNINGTON

The Evolution of the Flag

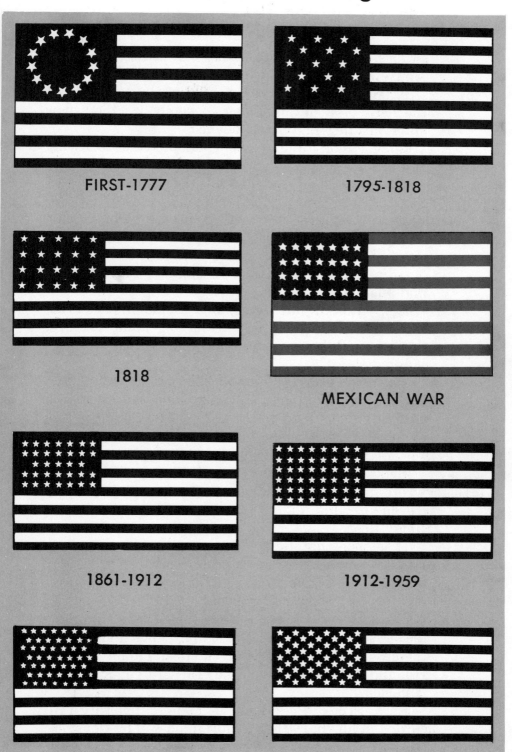

The Origin of Our Flag

stripes and a blue field with the crosses of Saint Andrew and Saint George.

After July 4, 1776, the people of the colonies felt the need of a national flag to symbolize their new spirit of unity and independence.

Congress on June 14, 1777, adopted the following resolution:—

"Resolved that the flag of the thirteen United States be thirteen stripes, alternate red and white; that the union be thirteen stars, white on a blue field." The significance of the colors was defined thus: "White signifies Purity and Innocence; Red, Hardiness and Valor; Blue, Vigilance, Perseverance and Justice."

Betsy Ross, a flag maker of Philadelphia, is credited by some historians with having made the first flag and with having suggested that the stars be five-pointed.

The home of Betsy Ross at 239 Arch Street, Philadelphia, is a National Shrine and the flag flies on a staff from her third floor window. Thousands of people of all nations visit this house, which is known as the Birthplace of Old Glory.

Betsy Ross had a grandson, William J. Canby, who wrote in 1857 that he was told the story as a boy of eleven by his eighty-four-year-old grandmother, Betsy Ross.

It is true that Betsy Ross was known as a flag-maker and that there is in the archives of the Navy an order to Elizabeth Ross "for making Ships Colors" for 14 pounds, 12 shillings and 2 pence, paid to her exactly two weeks before the Marine Committee's resolution of June 14th, 1777, which adopted the theme of the red and white striped Union Flag of Holland to the flag of the 13 United States of America.

Ezra Stiles, President of Yale University, recorded in his diary the resolution passed by Congress

The Origin of Our Flag

in 1777.

"The Congress have substituted a new Constella of 13 stars (instead of the union) in the Continental Colors."

On May 1st, 1795, our flag was changed to 15 stripes and 15 stars with the inclusion of Vermont (1791) and Kentucky (1792) into the Union.

It was this flag that was "so gallantly streaming" over Fort McHenry when Francis Scott Key wrote "The Star-Spangled Banner." The 15 striped, 15 starred flag was flying from 1795 to 1818.

On April 4th, 1818, Congress enacted the following law which is still in effect:—

"That the Flag of the United States be 13 horizontal stripes, alternate red and white, and that on the admission of every State into the Union, one star to be added on the Fourth of July next succeeding admission."

When the Flag Was First Flown in Battle

Fort Stanwix, New York, August 3, 1777. The city of Rome, N.Y. is now the spot where Fort Stanwix was situated. On August the 2nd, British and Indians attacked the fort which was defended by Col. Peter Gansevoort with 600 men. Lieutenant Col. Mellon arrived at the fort that afternoon, leading 200 men of the Ninth Massachusetts Regiment. They brought supplies and ammunition and also newspapers that carried accounts of the newly enacted flag resolution.

The fort was ransacked for material with which to make a flag patterned after the new national emblem. The soldiers gave up their white shirts. One of the wives of the men donated her red flannel petticoat and Captain Abraham Swartwout's blue cloth coat was donated to provide the blue field of the union.

Battle of Guilford Courthouse, March 15, 1781, is the first time the Stars and Stripes were carried by the North Carolina Militia of the American army in the Revolutionary War. It had 13 8-pointed stars.

Fort Miamis and Detroit were both occupied by the American army, led by General Anthony Wayne, on July 25, 1791. The American Flag and American rule arrived at the same time along the Great Lakes. A bronze historical marker close to the Detroit River front identifies the spot where the American Flag was first raised, and a letter, still preserved, was written by Dr. Charles Brown on September 28, 1796, who had arrived with the first advance detachment of troops on July 11. He wrote:—

"and the very staff that elevated their (The British flag) union now displays the stripes of America" (The "stripes" referred to may have been the flag of thirteen stripes, adorned by the figure of a rattlesnake, with the legend, "Don't Tread On Me." It could have meant the Stars and Stripes which were adopted in 1777.

The Flag and the U.S. Army

When Washington transferred his army from Boston to New York he carried the Grand Union Flag with him. July 9, 1776, after the first reading of the Declaration of Independence, he had it raised over his fortifications and headquarters. To confirm this, Admiral Lord Howe, Commander of British fleet then in New York harbor, wrote on July 25, 1776, "They have set up their standard in the fort upon the Southern end of the town (The Battery). Their colors are thirteen stripes of red and white alternately, with the English Union cantoned in the corner."

For the first six months of 1776 this flag was the flag of the United Colonies and on July 4th became the flag of the United States.

June 14, 1777, Congress in session in Philadelphia resolved: "That the Flag of the thirteen United States be 13 stripes, alternate red and white and that the union be 13 stars, white in a blue field, representing a new constellation."

There is no record that the Army was notified by Congress of this ruling. It also neglected to appropriate money for supplying flags to the Army. It was left to each regiment to supply its own flags.

Aug. 3, 1777, Stars and Stripes raised over Fort Stanwix (now Rome) New York. Lt. Col. Ward Willett wrote at the time: "The white stripes were cut out of ammunition shirts furnished by the soldiers, the blue out of the camlet cloak taken from the enemy at Peekskill; while the red stripes were made of different pieces of stuff procured from one and another of the garrison."

Jan. 13, 1794, flag bill was approved by President Washington. This was the first bill to receive the signature of the President.

"An Act making alterations in the Flag of the United States. Be it enacted, etc., that from and

The Flag and the U.S. Army

after 1st day of May, 1795, the Flag of the United States be 15 stripes, alternate red and white, and that the union be 15 stars, white in a blue field."

The Army had only begun to carry the Stars and Stripes as the national colors. When the Army was re-established in 1789 the national colors carried by the Army consisted of a blue field embroidered with an eagle. During the War of 1812 the flag carried by the various companies contained an eagle in whose breast was a striped shield. As each state was admitted to the Union, the stars around the eagle's head were rearranged to include the new star.

In 1834, the Stars and Stripes were supplied to the Artillery for the first time.

It was not until 1841 that the Infantry was first given permission to carry the Stars and Stripes.

The Flag resolutions of 1777 and the flag acts of 1794 and 1818 all prescribed white stars. Yet the Army used silver stars until after the Civil War when gold stars were used. For fifty years after the birth of the Stars and Stripes, the regimental flags used six-pointed stars as often as five.

The Army did not make its own flags, but purchased them from various flag makers, so the flags lacked uniformity.

The War Department, attempting to standardize the arrangement of the stars in the union of the flag, issued a War Department Order of March 18, 1896. It was signed by David S. Lamont, Secretary of War. It read:—

"The field or union of the National Flag in use in the Army will on and after July 4, 1896, consist of forty-five stars, in six rows, the first, third and fifth rows to have eight stars, and the second, fourth, and sixth rows seven stars each, in a blue field."

From that date on, the flags carried by all units of the Army were the same.

Our Navy and the Flag

The ships of the Colonial Fleet in the Delaware River flew the Grand Union Flag in 1775. (Sometimes called the Congress Colors.) It consisted of thirteen stripes, alternately red and white, representing the thirteen Colonies, with a blue field in the upper left hand corner bearing the crosses of St. George and St. Andrew, signifying union with the mother country.

After the Declaration of Independence, Colonial vessels were putting to sea to prey on British commerce. They flew the flags of the particular Colonies to which they belonged.

The first occasion upon which any American Flag floated over foreign territory was on March 3, 1776. Commodore Hopkins, of the Congress Fleet, organized an expedition against New Providence, in the Bahama Islands, for the purpose of seizing a quantity of powder stored there. Fort Nassau was taken and they commandeered a great quantity of military stores. These ships carried the standard which had a rattlesnake and the motto "Don't Tread on Me" and the thirteen striped flag.

John Paul Jones, a great hero of the Revolutionary Navy, hoisted the first truly American Flag. They called it the Grand Union Flag and the First Navy Ensign. It was used until it was superceded by the Stars and Stripes in 1777. Jones wrote:—

"It was my fortune, as the senior of the First Lieutenants, to hoist myself the Flag of America (I chose to do it with my own hands) the first time it was displayed."

On Sept. 4th, 1777, the first time the Navy went into action at sea, Captain Thomas Thompson in command of the Raleigh and the Alfred, sailed for France from Portsmouth. They captured the Nancy of the Windward Island Fleet. Later Thompson recorded this battle in his log:—

Our Navy and the Flag

"We up sails, out guns, hoisted Continental colours and bid them strike to the Thirteen United States . . . About a quarter of an hour all hands quitted quarters on board the British-Man-of-War."

April 24, 1778, John Paul Jones was in command of the Ranger, which conquered the British warship Drake. He wrote;—"I hoisted the American Stars," after the first U.S. Naval victory.

January 13, 1794, The Marine Committee of the Second Continental Congress presented the Resolution which was adopted for making the flag one of fifteen stars and fifteen stripes.

1801 the Bashaw of Tripoli declared war on the United States. Commodore Edward Preble was sent to the Mediterranean in command of a squadron. The frigate Philadelphia was captured by the Tripolitans. Lieutenant Stephen Decatur volunteered to destroy the captive frigate. He, with 74 comrades entered the harbor at night and blew up the ship.

Sept. 10, 1813, Oliver Hazard Perry (1785–1819) brother of Matthew C. Perry, was placed in command of the Naval force in Lake Erie, in the War of 1812. He fought the British from his flagship Lawrence which flew the flag with the words, "Don't Give Up the Ship." He destroyed the British fleet and sent the message, "We met the enemy and they are ours."

Matthew Calbraith Perry (1794–1858) served on his brother's ship the Revenge. He next served on the President which fired the first shot in the War of 1812.

In 1843 Perry was in command of the fleet which helped General Winfield Scott capture Vera Cruz in the Mexican War.

July 8, 1853 Perry arrived in Tokyo Bay, then called Yedo, to open Japanese ports to American ships.

David G. Farragut (1801–1870) our first Admiral, was famed for his saying, "I would see every

Our Navy and the Flag

man of you damned before I would raise my hand against that flag." He was stationed on the Hartford during the battle of Mobile Bay. He said:—

"Damn the torpedoes! Full speed ahead!"

Honors to the Colors—Naval ships not underway hoist the national ensign at the flagstaff aft at 8 a.m. and lower it at sunset. The union jack, likewise, is hoisted smartly and lowered slowly and is never allowed to touch the deck. At both morning and evening "colors," "Attention" is sounded, and all officers and men topside face the ensign and render the salute. At shore stations and, in peacetime, on board large vessels where a band is present, the National Anthem is played during the ceremonies. In the absence of a band, the bugler, if available, sounds "To the Colors" at the morning ceremonies and "Retreat" at sunset formalities. When a Naval ship is underway, the ensign usually is flown both day and night at the main mast and the jack is not hoisted.

During "colors," a boat underway within sight or hearing of the ceremony either lies to or proceeds at the slowest safe speed. The boat officer—or in his absence the coxswain—stands and salutes except when dangerous to do so. Other persons in the boat remain seated or standing and do not salute. Vehicles within sight or hearing of "colors" are stopped. Persons riding in vehicles sit at attention. The person in charge of a military vehicle (but someone other than the driver) renders the hand salute.

When a vessel under the flag of a nation formally recognized by the Government of the United States salutes a ship of our Navy by dipping her ensign, the salute is returned dip for dip.

In half-masting the design, it is first raised to the truck or peak and then lowered to half-mast. Before being lowered from half-mast, the ensign is first raised to the truck or peak and lowered with the usual ceremonies.

Old Glory and the U.S. Marines

The United States Marine Corps distributes a booklet on "How to Respect and Display Our Flag," to every Marine recruit. It describes the achievements of the Marines since the beginnings of that organization in 1775. Among the highlights in Marine Corps records when the Marines carried the flag to remote places are the following:

Landed in the Bahamas on March 3, 1776, on their first expedition, bringing with them the Grand Union flag and a Rattlesnake flag.

Helped to defend the flag in the sea fight between the U.S.S. Bon Homme Richard and the H.M.S. Serapis, September 23, 1779, when John Paul Jones made his defiant retort: "I have not yet begun to fight."

Carried the Stars and Stripes to the "Shores of Tripoli" where it was hoisted at Derne in North Africa, April 27, 1805, the first time our flag was flown over a fortress of the Old World.

Took part in the defense of Fort McHenry during the night of September 13, 1814, where, on the following morning, our flag inspired Francis Scott Key to write the Star-Spangled Banner.

Raised Old Glory over the Custom House at Monterey, California, while U.S. Naval vessels in the harbor fired a twenty-one gun salute on July 7, 1846.

Marched with General Quitman's division when it entered the "Halls of Montezuma," in Mexico City, and hoisted the Stars and Stripes on September 14, 1847.

Unfurled the national flag at Guantanamo Bay, Cuba, when they landed there on June 10, 1898, and held the surrounding terrain as a base for the U.S. Navy.

Accepted surrender of the island of Guam when, along with the bluejackets of the U.S. Navy, they witnessed the lowering of the Spanish flag, and raised the Stars and Stripes, June 20, 1898.

Took part in the special ceremonies when the Stars and Stripes were first raised over American Samoa

Old Glory and the U.S. Marines

in the Samoan Islands on April 17, 1900.

As a part of the Allied Relief Expedition which raised the seige of the Allied Legations in China during the Boxer Rebellion, in July and August, 1900, hoisted the Stars and Stripes over the Walled City of Tientsin in July, 1900 and over the Tartar City (Pekin) wall in August, and later hoisted it on the ruins of Pekin's Chien Men Gate as a signal to the other Allied Forces that the Imperial City had fallen.

Fought side by side with the bluejackets of the U.S. Navy when they came ashore at Vera Cruz, Mexico, on April 21, 1914, later raising the national flag at a special ceremony.

Throughout the United States, at U.S. bases overseas, at American Embassies in foreign lands, United States Marines perform the official honors to the American flag. Around the globe the Stars and Stripes fly at more than 500 stations where Marines are on duty.

The Stars and Stripes which flew over the United States Capitol on December 8, 1941, when the United States declared war on Japan and on December 11 when we declared war on Germany and Italy, has indeed proved to be the "flag of liberation." This same flag went with President Roosevelt to Algiers, Casablanca, and other historic places, and flew over the conquered cities of Rome, Berlin and Tokyo.

The Stars and Stripes that flew over Pearl Harbor on December 7, 1941, rippled above the Big Three conference at Potsdam. This same flag was flying over the White House on August 14, 1945, when the Japanese accepted surrender terms.

The famous picture of Marines raising the flag on Iwo Jima was taken by Marine photographer, Joe Rosenthal, and later made into a monument by sculptor Felix De Weldon. It is in Arlington, Virginia, as Memorial to the U.S. Marine Corps. The flag flies there day and night by order of President John F. Kennedy.

The U.S. Coast Guard and the Flag

The U.S. Coast Guard is the oldest seagoing service in the United States. On August 4, 1790, President Washington signed a bill to purchase ten boats to be used to guard the coast against smugglers.

In the beginning the service was called the Revenue Marines; later it was called the Revenue Cutter Service. In 1848 it was renamed the United States Coast Guard. Although its name was changed it kept its identity as an organization.

The father of the Coast Guard was Alexander Hamilton, the first Secretary of the Treasury. It was he who asked Congress to provide a fleet of armed cutters to insure the collection of tonnage dues and import duties from vessels entering U.S. waters and to enforce the customs laws.

In 1796 the ten original cutters were replaced with bigger ships which carried more and better guns, and the evolution which lead to the 20th century Coast Guard was under way.

On April 6, 1917, at the start of World War I, the Coast Guard had 15 cruising cutters, 200 officers and 5,000 men. The naval action was almost exclusively undersea warfare. The Coast Guard convoyed cargo ships and screened transports carrying troops.

In World War II the Coast Guard hit its peak strength. It had 802 vessels of its own over 65 feet and manned 351 Navy and 288 Army craft. Shore stations increased from 1,096 to 17,074. At the end of June, 1945, personnel numbered 171,168.

The Coast Guard Flag or Ensign was designed in 1799 by Oliver Wolcott. It had 16 perpendicular stripes, alternating red and white with the arms of the United States in the union of the ensign, blue on white field.

In 1927 the Coast Guard Seal was put into this flag centered on the middle of the 7th red stripe. It is the only service flag that has been changed only twice during the history of our country.

The Star-Spangled Banner

Francis Scott Key (1779–1843) who wrote "The Star-Spangled Banner," the National Anthem of the United States, was born in Frederick (now Carroll) County, Maryland. He was educated at St. John's College, Annapolis, Md., and practiced law in Frederick.

Key was living in Washington, D.C., at the time of the War of 1812. He received permission from President James Madison to ask the British to release his friend, Dr. William Beanes, who had been taken prisoner.

On Sept. 13, 1814, Key was rowed out to a British ship in Baltimore harbor to ask for the release of his friend. The release was secured, but Key was detained on ship overnight during the shelling of the fort. The British were afraid if they released him, that Key might give news of the British strength to the garrison. When morning came and he saw the American flag still flying, he began to write a poem to commemorate the event. He must have written the words to the tune of "Anacreon in Heaven" which was an old British song, supposedly written by John Stafford Smith, a British composer.

The song gained wide popularity and was sung at many patriotic gatherings before it became officially the National Anthem by an Act of Congress in 1931.

The Star-Spangled Banner that waved triumphantly over Fort McHenry and which inspired Key's poem, was ordered made by Brig. Gen. John Stricker. It was made by Mrs. Mary Pickersgill, assisted by her daughter and two nieces.

The flag was originally forty-two feet long but was shortened by stress of battle and relic seekers. Each stripe measured nearly two feet in width, and the five-pointed stars, two feet from point to point. The flag was made in sections, and because of its great length, the women had to remove it from their home

The Star-Spangled Banner

and take it to the loft of a brewery in order to set in the canton with the stars. This flag has been restored and is now in the Museum of History and Technology, Wash., D.C.

O say, can you see, by the dawn's early light,
What so proudly we hail'd at the twilight's last gleaming?
Whose broad stripes and bright stars, thro' the perilous fight,
O'er the ramparts we watch'd, were so gallantly streaming?
And the rockets' red glare, the bombs bursting in air,
Gave proof thro' the night that our flag was still there.
O say, does that star-spangled banner yet wave
O'er the land of the free and the home of the brave?

On the shore dimly seen thro' the mists of the deep,
Where the foe's haughty host in dread silence reposes,
What is that which the breeze, o'er the towering steep,
As it fitfully blows, half conceals, half discloses?
Now it catches the gleam of the morning's first beam,
In full glory reflected, now shines on the stream;
'Tis the star-spangled banner: O, long may it wave
O'er the land of the free and the home of the brave!

And where is that band who so vauntingly swore

The Star-Spangled Banner

*That the havoc of war and the battle's
   confusion,
A home and a country should leave us no more?
Their blood has wash'd out their foul footsteps'
   pollution.
No refuge could save the hireling and slave
From the terror of flight or the gloom of the
   grave:
And the star-spangled banner in triumph doth
   wave
O'er the land of the free and the home of the
   brave.*

*O thus be it ever when free-men shall stand
Between their lov'd home and the war's
   desolation;
Blest with vict'ry and peace, may the heav'n-
   rescued land
Praise the Pow'r that hath made and preserv'd
   us a nation!
Then conquer we must, when our cause it is
   just,
And this be our motto: "In God is our Trust!"
And the star-spangled banner in triumph shall
   wave
O'er the land of the free and the home of the
   brave!*

The Man Who Established the Flag

Peter Hercules Wendover (1768–1834) was born in New York City. He received a liberal schooling and held several offices in New York. He was a Delegate to the State Constitutional Convention in 1796, a Member of The State Assembly in 1804, and was elected as a Democrat to the 14th, 15th, and 16th Congress as a representative from New York. He served the Congress from 1815 to 1821.

It was P. H. Wendover, the little bulldog of the Congress, who made it his life's work to get the Congress to pass an act to establish the Flag of the United States. He pointed out that flags bearing anything from nine to eighteen stripes were then flying in the city of Washington, D.C.

This was the day before typewriters, and Congressman Wendover wrote hundreds of letters to everyone who was influential, begging them to support his dream to establish the flag. Here are some excerpts from his hand written letters:—

Washington, Feb. 13, 1817—*"The flag is yet on the table; I know not when it will get to the anvil. I find the flag proposition is almost universally approved of, but fear the standard will have to lie over till next season . . ."*

Washington, Mar. 24, 1818—*"This day the first call on the docket was the 'Star-Spangled Banner.' I moved to go in committee on the bill. General Smith moved to discharge the Committee of the Whole, and postpone the bill indefinitely. I appealed to that gentleman and the House to know if they were willing to thus neglect the banner of freedom . . . General Smith's motion was negatived by almost a unanimous vote, and we hoisted the 'striped bunting' (to lend interest to the debate on the bill, Mr. Wendover had hoisted striped bunting).*

"After I had made a few observations and sat down, Mr. Poindexter moved to strike out twenty

The Man Who Established the Flag

stars and insert seven, with a view to have stripes for the old and stars for the new States; motion rejected nearly unanimously. Mr. Folger then moved to strike out twenty and insert thirteen, to restore the original flag; his motion was also negatived by a similar vote ... the committee rose and reported the bill without amendment, and the House ordered it engrossed for a third reading tomorrow by almost a unanimous vote.

"It was remarked by many that the subject came up in good time, as our Flag almost blew away with the severe storm, which on Saturday was almost a hurricane. It is now completely 'ragged bunting,' and I fear we shall have to sit a part of the session without the 'Star-Spangled Banner' over our heads."

"P.S. Mar. 25—Having written the within after the close of the last mail, I kept this open to inform you further as to the 'Star-Spangled Banner.' The bill had its third reading this day, a little before twelve o'clock, and passed with about two or three 'noes' ... Mr. Taylor moved to amend the title of the bill, and instead of "Alter," it is now, 'A bill to Establish the Flag of the United States."

The bill was sent to the Senate and a vote of concurrence was passed on March 31, 1818. The bill was signed by President Monroe, Apr. 4, 1818.

This is the law:—

"**An Act to Establish the Flag of the United States. Sect. 1. Be it enacted, etc., That from and after the fourth day of July next, the flag of the United States be thirteen horizontal stripes, alternate red and white; that the union have twenty stars, white in a blue field. Sect. 2. Be it further enacted, That on the admission of every new State into the Union, one star be added to the union of the flag; and that such addition shall take effect on the fourth of July next succeeding such admission.**"

Dates of Admission of States

Order of Admission	State	Date Ratified or Admitted	Flag Design	Dates in Use	No. of Stars	No. of Stripes
1	Del.	Dec. 7, 1787	1st	1777–95	13	13
2	Penn.	Dec. 12, 1787				
3	N.J.	Dec. 18, 1787				
4	Ga.	Jan. 2, 1788				
5	Conn.	Jan. 9, 1788				
6	Mass.	Feb. 6, 1788				
7	Md.	Apr. 28, 1788				
8	S.C.	May 23, 1788				
9	N.H.	Jun. 21, 1788				
10	Va.	Jun. 25, 1788				
11	N.Y.	Jul. 26, 1788				
12	N.C.	Nov. 21, 1789				
13	R.I.	May 29, 1790				
14	Vt.	Mar. 4, 1791				
15	Ky.	Jun. 1, 1792				
16	Tenn.	Jun. 1, 1796				
17	Ohio	Mar. 1, 1803	2nd	1795 to 1818	15	15
18	La.	Apr. 30, 1812				
19	Ind.	Dec. 11, 1816				
20	Miss.	Dec. 10, 1817	3rd	1818	20	13
21	Ill.	Dec. 3, 1818	4th	1819	21	13
22	Ala.	Dec. 14, 1819	5th	1820	23	13
23	Me.	Mar. 15, 1820				
24	Mo.	Aug. 10, 1821	6th	1822	24	13
25	Ark.	Jun. 15, 1836	7th	1836	25	13
26	Mich.	Jan. 26, 1837	8th	1837	26	13
27	Fla.	Mar. 3, 1845	9th	1845	27	13
28	Tex.	Dec. 29, 1845	10th	1846	28	13
29	Iowa	Dec. 28, 1846	11th	1847	29	13
30	Wis.	May 29, 1848	12th	1848	30	13
31	Calif.	Sep. 9, 1850	13th	1851	31	13
32	Minn.	May 11, 1858	14th	1858	32	13
33	Ore.	Feb. 14, 1859	15th	1849	33	13
34	Kan.	Jan. 29, 1861	16th	1861	34	13
35	W. Va.	Jun. 20, 1863	17th	1863	35	13
36	Nev.	Oct. 31, 1864	18th	1865	36	13
37	Neb.	Mar. 1, 1867	19th	1867	37	13
38	Colo.	Aug. 1, 1876	20th	1877	38	13
39	N.D.					
40	S.D.	Nov. 2, 1889				
41	Mont.	Nov. 8, 1889	21st	1890	43	13
42	Wash.	Nov. 11, 1889				

Dates of Admission of States

Order of Admission	State	Date Ratified or Admitted	Flag Design	Dates in Use	No. of Stars	No. of Stripes
43	Idaho	Jul. 3, 1890				
44	Wyo.	Jul. 10, 1890	22nd	1891	44	13
45	Utah	Jan. 4, 1896	23rd	1896	45	13
46	Okla.	Nov. 16, 1907	24th	1908	46	13
47	N.M.	Jan. 6, 1912	25th	1912	48	13
48	Ariz.	Feb. 14, 1912				
49	Alas.	Jan. 3, 1959	26th	1959	49	13
50	Haw.	Aug. 21, 1959	27th	1960	50	13

U.S. Flag Foundation

The first American Flag Association was organized in 1898 in New York. It was a union of flag committees of the various patriotic societies of the U.S. fostering public sentiment in favor of honoring the flag and preserving it from desecration through legal means. This association continued active until 1936.

The U.S. Flag Foundation was incorporated in 1942 to carry on the work of the American Flag Association. Its president is Lawrence Phelps Tower and its address is 115 East 86th Street, New York, N.Y. 10028.

Its aims are to help prepare the youth of America for the duties and responsibilities of citizenship, combat all influences hostile to the Constitution and to advance the true meaning of civil and religious liberty by creating appreciation and love for the American way of life under the stars and stripes.

The Father of Flag Day

The popular observance of the anniversary of the adoption of the flag was of slow growth.

Three states claimed one of their own residents was responsible for the observance of Flag Day on June 14th, the anniversary of the day the Continental Congress adopted the Flag of the United States in 1777.

Bernard J. Cigrand (1866–1932) was a school teacher in Waubeka, Wisconsin, and he spent years trying to get Congress to declare June 14th National Flag Day. Finally, in 1877, the Congress of the United States requested that the flag be flown from all public buildings on June 14th. Although Congress did not designate it as an official national holiday, it was widely observed.

The National Fraternal Flag Day Foundation in Neenah, Wisconsin was founded in 1948 to preserve as a shrine the school house and grounds where the birth of Flag Day occurred on June 14, 1885.

The first state to establish the June 14th, Flag Day as a legal holiday was Pennsylvania on May 7th, 1937.

New York State claims that in 1889, George Bolch, the principal of a free kindergarten for the poor, decided to hold patriotic exercises on that day. His action attracted the attention of the State Department of Education and not long afterward the State Legislature passed a law providing that:—"It shall be the duty of the State Superintendent of Public Schools to prepare a program making special provisions for observance in the public schools of Lincoln's Birthday, Washington's Birthday, Memorial Day and Flag Day, June 14th."

Eugene Meyer Jr. in his book, **Festivals in the U.S.A.** gives the title of Father of Flag Day to a William T. Kerr, who was credited with founding

The Father of Flag Day

the American Flag Day Association in 1888 while he was still a school boy in Pittsburgh, Pa.

In 1893 in Philadelphia, the Mayor, in response to a resolution of the Society of Colonial Dames, ordered the display of the flag on the public buildings of the city. Mrs. Elizabeth Duane Gillespie, a direct descendant of Benjamin Franklin and at that time President of the Colonial Dames of Pennsylvania, also proposed that the day be known as Flag Day and that the flag be displayed by all citizens on their residences and on all business places as well as on public buildings. But this was before Women's Liberation movement, and little notice was taken of it.

In 1897 the Governor of New York issued a proclamation ordering the display of the flag over all public buildings in the state on Flag Day.

President Wilson in 1916 and President Coolidge in 1927 issued proclamations asking that June 14 be observed as National Flag Day.

Finally, Congress on August 3rd, 1949, gave its approval to the project. In a joint resolution it resolved:

"That the 14th day of June of each year is hereby designated as Flag Day and the President of the United States is authorized and requested to issue annually a proclamation calling upon all officials of the Government to display the Flag of the United States on all Government buildings on such day, urging the people to observe the day as an anniversary of the adoption on June 14, 1777, by the Continental Congress of the United States of the Stars and Stripes as the official Flag of the United States of America."

President Harry Truman signed the measure into law the same day, August 3rd, 1949.

The Origin of Loyalty Day

May 1st of each year is designated as Loyalty Day by Congressional Act 85-529 of 1958.

The Veterans of Foreign Wars claims that it was due to their efforts that the bill was passed.

The V.F.W.'s fight to obtain federal government recognition of May 1st as "Loyalty Day" began with the adoption of a resolution at the Golden Jubilee V.F.W. National Convention in Miami in 1949.

Representative James E. Van Zandt, Pennsylvania, three-times Commander-in-Chief of the Veterans of Foreign Wars, launched the bill in Congress in 1954. His bill passed the House but not the Senate. Undaunted, he reintroduced the measure in 1955; and Congress approved it, but simply designated May 1, 1955 as "Loyalty Day."

The V.F.W. continued to push the bill, and finally in 1958 the bill was adopted as Public Law 529.

Since its passage, Loyalty Day has been gaining impetus across the land as millions of Americans participate in programs to promote loyalty.

Flag Plaza Foundation

The Flag Plaza stands proudly at the base of Pittsburgh's Golden Triangle. In front of the whitestone building are five flag poles, eighty feet tall.

The fifty-star Flag of the United States of America waves majestically atop the highest pole. Four other banners flank Old Glory. The crest of the City of Pittsburgh, the colors of the Commonwealth of Pennsylvania, and the ensign of the Boy Scouts of America. The fourth flag is one of thirty-one historic flags.

It was given to the youth of America by Vivian W. Lehman in memory of her husband, Chester H. Lehman. It was dedicated on Independence Day, 1968 and is entrusted to the Allegheny Trails Council, Boy Scouts of America, of which Mr. Lehman was a Scout Leader. It serves 1,300 scout units.

The Pledge of Allegiance

Francis Bellamy (1855–1931) wrote the Pledge for the observance of the 400th Anniversary of the discovery of America by Columbus. He was working on a journal for juveniles, called Youth's Companion. James B. Upham was the editor and they worked closely together. He went to the paper in 1891.

His job on the paper was to promote patriotism and the flying of the flag over the public schools. He was made Chairman of the executive committee for the National Public School Celebration of Columbus Day in 1892. He felt every public and private school in the land should fly the flag.

Bellamy visited President Benjamin Harrison in Washington to ask him to endorse the idea of a flag over every school house and the teaching of patriotism in all the schools. On June 21st, 1892 President Harrison signed the Proclamation that said, "Let the National Flag float over every school house in the country and the exercises be such as shall impress upon our youth the patriotic duties of American citizenship!"

Francis Bellamy wrote these now famous words, first printed in Youth's Companion, Sept. 8, 1892:—

"I pledge allegiance to the Flag of the United States and to the Republic for which it stands, one Nation, indivisible, with liberty and justice for all."

At the Second National Flag Conference held in Washington, D.C. on Flag Day, 1924, they added the words **"of America."**

A further change was made in the Pledge by House Joint Resolution 243, approved by President Eisenhower on June 14, 1954. This amended the language by adding the words **"under God,"** so that it now reads,

"one Nation under God, indivisible, with liberty and justice for all."

The American's Creed

by William Tyler Page

"I believe in the United States of America as a Government of the People, by the people, for the people; whose just powers are derived from the consent of the governed; a democracy in a republic, a sovereign Nation of many sovereign States; a perfect union, one and inseparable, established upon those principles of freedom, equality, justice, and humanity for which American patriots sacrificed their lives and fortunes. I therefore believe it is my duty to my country to love it; to support its constitution; to obey its laws; to respect its flag; and to defend it against all enemies."

The American's Creed was written in 1918 in the course of a nation-wide contest.

The then-Mayor of Baltimore, James H. Preston, offered a reward of $1,000 for the winning statement. The meaning of the Creed is best expressed by the author: "The American's Creed is the summing up in one hundred words, of the basic principles of American political faith. It is not an expression of individual opinion upon the obligations and duties of American citizenship or with respect to its rights and privileges. It is a summary of the fundamental principles of American political faith as set forth in its greatest documents, its worthiest traditions, and by its greatest leaders."

William Tyler Page (1868–1942) worked for the Government at the Capitol all of his life, starting in 1881. For twenty-two consecutive years he led the assembled Continental Congresses of the Daughters of the American Revolution in reciting the Creed. He died October 18, 1942, the day after he led the recitation of the American's Creed at the 50th anniversary celebration of the Pledge of Allegiance to the Flag.

Names Given to Our Flag

Poets, patriots and composers have given endearing names to our National Flag. The best known are:

OLD GLORY—William Driver (1803–1886) As the flag of the United States was hoisted to the masthead of his brig, he said, "I name thee OLD GLORY." This is the first time that the flag was called OLD GLORY.

THE STAR-SPANGLED BANNER was the title of the song that Francis Scott Key wrote that night off Fort McHenry when he watched the bombardment of the fort by the British in 1814. The poem was set to an old English tune and was declared our National Anthem by Congress in 1931.

THE STARS AND STRIPES—George Henry Preble in 1880 wrote in his "History of the United States of America" . . . "When the Stars and Stripes went down at Sumter, they went up in every town and country in the loyal states."

STARRY FLAG—George Frederick Root (1820–1895) was most likely the first song writer to use the word STARRY in describing our flag. In 1862 he wrote the song;—"Tramp! Tramp! Tramp!

> *The boys are marching*
> *Cheer up comrades, they will come*
> *and beneath the STARRY FLAG*
> *We shall breathe the air again*
> *In the free land of our own beloved home."*

FREEDOM'S BANNER—Joseph Rodman Drake (1795–1820) wrote a poem called "The American Flag"

> *"Flag of the free heart's hope and home,*
> *By Angel-hands to valor given,*
> *Thy stars have lit the welkin dome,*
> *And all thy hues were born in heaven.*

Names Given to Our Flag

Forever float that standard sheet,
Where breathes the foe but falls before us,
With Freedom's soil beneath our feet,
And FREEDOM'S BANNER streaming o'er us!

Famous Songs About the Flag

COLUMBIA, THE GEM OF THE OCEAN

This stirring song was first sung in 1843 by David T. Shaw, in Philadelphia. Thomas a Becket, an actor friend, wrote the words and music.

Columbia, the gem of the ocean,
The home of the brave and the free,—
The shrine of each patriot's devotion,
A world offers homage to thee.
Thy banners make tyranny tremble,
When Liberty's form stands in view;
Thy banners make tyranny tremble,
When borne by the red, white and blue;
(Chorus) When borne by the red, white and blue,
When borne by the red, white and blue,
Thy banners make tyranny tremble,
When borne by the red, white and blue.
When war winged its wide desolation,
And threatened the land to deform,—
The ark then of freedom's foundation,
Columbia rode safe thro' the storm;
With her garlands of vict'ry around her,
When so proudly she bore her bold crew,
With her flag floating proudly before us,
The boast of the red, white and blue.
(Repeat Chorus)
The Star-Spangled banner bring hither,
O'er Columbia's true sons let it wave,—
May the wreaths they have won never wither,
Nor its stars cease to shine on the brave.
May the service united ne'er sever,
But hold to their colors so true;
The Army and Navy Forever,
Three cheers for the red, white and blue.
(Chorus) Three cheers for the red, white and blue
Three cheers for the red, white and blue
The Army and Navy forever,
Three cheers for the red, white and blue.

Famous Songs About the Flag

George Frederick Root (1820–1895) was an American composer. He is best remembered for his patriotic songs: "The Battle Cry of Freedom" and "Tramp, Tramp, Tramp, the Boys are Marching," which were inspired by the War between the States.

THE BATTLE CRY OF FREEDOM

Yes, we'll rally round the flag, boys,
We'll rally once again,
Shouting the battle cry of Freedom.
We will rally from the hillside,
We'll gather from the plain,
Shouting the battle cry of Freedom.
(Chorus) It's Freedom forever. Hurrah, Boys, Hurrah!
    Down with the shackle and up with the star!
    While we rally round the flag, boys,
    We'll rally once again,
    Shouting the battle cry of Freedom!

George M. Cohan (1878–1942) wrote the words and music for "You're a Grand Old Flag" in 1906. He introduced it in the musical, "George Washington, Jr." Cohan's idea for this song came after talking to a veteran who told him he had been a colorbearer during Pickett's charge at Gettysburg. Pointing to an American flag he said, "She's a grand old flag."

YOU'RE A GRAND OLD FLAG

You're a grand old flag,
You're a high flying flag,
And forever in peace may you wave.
You're the emblem of the land I love,
The home of the free and the brave.
Every heart beats true under red, white and blue,
Where there's never a boast or brag.
But should auld acquaintance be forgot,
Keep your eye on the grand old flag.

Famous Paintings of the Flag

Col. John Trumbull (1756–1843) was the great painter of the Revolution. He was particularly interested in the flags carried by the victors and the vanquished. In every one of his battle scenes the Flag of the United States is the focal point.

He knew and painted the first six Presidents of the United States.

He was born in Lebanon, Connecticut, the son of the Governor of Connecticut. When the Revolutionary War was on he became aide-de-camp for a short time to General Washington.

When the war was over he sailed to England and studied painting with Benjamin West from 1780 to 1789. Then he returned to America and travelled up and down the eastern seaboard to make sketches of all the important men in the armed forces and government. He then went back to England.

He returned to America in 1804 and brought with him the great canvases that he had painted in London showing the moments of defeat of the British forces. Among the most famous are:

(1) The Surrender of Lord Cornwallis at Yorktown, Virginia Oct. 19, 1781. The sketch he made of this surrender was painted half life size. It is in the Capitol Building, Washington, D.C.

(2) Death of Gen. Mercer at the Battle of Princeton, N.J., Jan. 3rd, 1777. Shows our flag with 13 stars and 13 stripes. Original is at Yale University, New Haven, Connecticut.

(3) Surrender of Gen. Burgoyne at Saratoga, N.Y., Oct. 17th, 1777. The original is in the Rotunda in the Capitol in Washington, D.C. The flag has 13 stars and 13 stripes.

(4) Transferring the Louisiana Territory from France to America in New Orleans on Dec. 20, 1803. In Cabildo Louisiana State Museum, New Orleans. This flag has 15 stripes and 15 stars.

Famous Paintings of the Flag

Charles Wilson Peale (1741–1827) was noted for his portraits of soldiers and statesmen of the Revolution. He was born in Chestertown, Md. and studied with Benjamin West in London. He returned to the U.S. to fight with the American Army during the Revolutionary War. He painted fourteen portraits of George Washington. When he painted Washington at the Battle of Trenton, the American flag in the picture had 13 stars arranged in a circle. In other battle scenes he painted the flag with the stars arranged in a rectangle.

Rembrandt Peale (1778–1869) was the son of Charles Peale. He too studied in London with Benjamin West. When he returned to the U.S. he settled in Baltimore, Md. and had a studio there, which later became the Peale Museum. It is an historical museum with many pictures by Peale and is run by the City of Baltimore. Peale was noted as a portrait painter and also did many historical scenes.

G. H. Weisgerber, painted the famous picture of Betsy Ross showing the flag to General Washington, George Ross and Robert Morris in 1893. He called this picture "Birth of Our Nation's Flag." Hundreds of thousands of copies of this picture spread across the land. The flag in this picture had 13 stars arranged in a circle.

Archibald Willard, in 1875, painted the famous picture "The Spirit of '76." This flag also had the stars arranged in a circle. Willard was an Ohio carriage painter who designed this picture which he called "Yankee Doodle." He painted it to decorate a platform to celebrate the Centennial in Philadelphia. He evidently had trouble drawing feet, and so although there are six people in the picture, only four feet are showing! However it became a popular picture with the public and almost every American citizen of that day had a copy of it.

The American Flag

by Joseph Rodman Drake

Joseph Rodman Drake was born in 1795 and died of consumption when he was 25 years old in 1820.

He received his medical degree in 1816 and wrote poetry in his spare time. On his death-bed he ordered his poems destroyed. Fortunately, his daughter and his friend, Fitz-Green Halleck, published his poems; and Halleck wrote the last quatrain of "'The American Flag," his best-loved poem.

When Freedom, from her mountain height
Unfurled her standard to the air,
She tore the azure robe of night,
And set the stars of glory there!
She mingled with its gorgeous dyes
The milky baldric of the skies,
And striped its pure, celestial white
with streakings of the morning light;
Then, from his mansion in the sun,
She called her eagle-bearer down,
And gave into his mighty hand
The symbol of her chosen land.

Flag of the brave! thy folds shall fly
The sign of hope and triumph high!
When speaks the signal-trumpet tone,
And the long line comes gleaming on,
Ere yet the life-blood, warm and wet,
Has dimmed the glistening bayonet,
Each soldier eye shall brightly turn
To where thy sky-born glories burn,
And as his springing steps advance,
Catch war and vengeance from the glance;

And when the cannon-mouthings loud
Heave in wild wreaths the battle-shroud

The American Flag

And gory sabres rise and fall,
Like shoots of flame on midnight's pall;
Then shall thy meteor-glances glow,
And cowering foes shall sink beneath
Each gallant arm that strikes below
That lovely messenger of death.

Flag of the seas! on ocean wave
Thy stars shall glitter o'er the brave;
When death, careering on the gale,
Sweeps darkly round the bellied sail,
And frighted waves rush wildly back
Before the broadside's reeling rack,
Each dying wanderer of the sea
Shall look at once to heaven and thee,
And smile to see thy splendors fly
In triumph o'er his closing eye.

Flag of the free heart's hope and home,
By angel hands to valor given!
Thy stars have lit the welkin dome,
And all thy hues were born in heaven.
Forever float that standard sheet!
Where breathes the foe but falls before us,
When Freedom's soil beneath our feet,
And Freedom's banner streaming o'er us!"

(the last 4 lines by Halleck. Drake's were thus:—)

"And fixed as yonder orb divine,
That saw thy bannered blaze unfurled,
Shall thy proud stars resplendent shine,
The guard and glory of the world."

A Toast to the Flag

by John Jay Daly

1.
Here's to the Red of It—
There's not a thread of it,
No, nor a shred of it
In all the spread of it
   From foot to head
But heroes bled for it,
Faced steel and lead for it,
Precious blood shed for it,
   Bathing it Red!

2.
Here's to the White of It—
Thrilled by the sight of it,
Who knows the right of it
But feels the might of it
   Through day and night?
Womanhood's care for it
Made manhood dare for it;
Purity's pray'r for it
   Keeps it so White!

3.
Here's to the Blue of It—
Beauteous view of it,
Heavenly hue of it,
Star-spangled dew of it
   Constant and true;
Diadems gleam for it,
States stand supreme for it,
Liberty's beam for it
   Brightens the Blue!

4.
Here's to the Whole of It—
Stars, stripes and pole of it,
Body and soul of it,
O, and the roll of it,
   Sun shining through;
Hearts in accord for it
Swear by the sword for it,
Thanking the Lord for it,
   Red, White and Blue!

From John Jay Daly's book "Government U.S.A." A Comprehensive Review. Printed by Reese Press Baltimore, Maryland, 1954.
   Permission granted to use A Toast To The Flag by J. J. Daly, Aug. 9, 1970.

Flag of Our Fathers

by John Jay Daly

They burnt the flag of our country
In frantic remonstrance one day.
They ripped the flag from its masthead
And watched all its beauty decay;
Reduced to a heap of ashes,
Defiled by them, stomped under foot—
Old Glory—flag of our fathers—
Lay smothered in dust and in soot.
Almight God may forgive those
Who performed this ignoble act,
But few mortal men condone them,
Aware of the glorious fact
That others bled for our nation,
Armed with rifle, cannon and sword,
True to the Star-Spangled Banner
While praying for strength from the Lord.
Their heirs revere the Stars and Stripes
Wherever that emblem may wave,
A symbol of mankind's shelter,
The home of the free and the brave,
The flag of mighty immortals
Who, coming from different lands,
Guard us in spirit forever,
As long as America stands.
So, breathe a prayer of thanksgiving
For heroes who, down through the years,
Gave all they had for our country—
Their lives—precious blood, sweat and tears.
Listen: You'll hear, as in echo,
Their voices lamenting the lag
Of patriot's dreams as they plead:
"In God's name, stop burning the flag!"

This poem first appeared in the Disabled American Veteran's Magazine in September, 1967, after students burned flags to protest the U.S. War in Viet Nam. Reprinted by permission.

Famous Stories About the Flag

Barbara Frietchie of Frederick, Maryland, was a patriotic woman who risked her life to save the flag. John Greenleaf Whittier wrote a poem about her, based on a magazine account first published in the Atlantic Monthly in 1863.

According to the story, the men of Frederick hauled down the flag as Confederate troops under General Stonewall Jackson approached. Barbara Frietchie set the flag in her window. She defied the soldiers, and Whittier put these words in her mouth; —" 'Shoot if you must this old gray head, But spare your country's flag,' she said."

Jackson was moved by her appeal and ordered his men to move on. A tablet marks the spot where the incident occurred.

Edward Everett Hale wrote a novel called "The Man Without a Country," about a man named Philip Nolan who was an officer in the army. He was court-martialed and during his trial exclaimed that he never wanted to hear of the United States again. He was put on a ship with instructions that no one was ever to give him any news of his country again. He spent fifty years of his life at sea. On his deathbed he said, "I know I am dying. I am sure there is not in America—God Bless her!—a more loyal man than I. There cannot be a man who loved the old flag as I do, or prays for it as I do. There are thirty-four stars in it now ... I thank God for that."

He asked that his tombstone be enscribed: "Philip Nolan, Lieutenant in the Army of the United States. He loved his country as no other man has loved her, but no man deserved less at her hands."

So many readers believed Hale's story that he put a notice in subsequent editions that it was based entirely on his imagination.

The Makers of the Flag

by Franklin K. Lane

Franklin K. Lane, then Secretary of the Interior, wrote an oration on "Makers of the Flag." It was delivered on Flag Day, 1914, before the employees of the Department of the Interior, Washington, D.C.

"This morning, as I passed into the Land Office, the Flag dropped me a most cordial salutation; and from its rippling folds I heard it say; 'Good Morning, Mr. Flag-Maker.'

"I beg your pardon, Old Glory," I said, "aren't you mistaken? I am not the President of the United States, nor a member of Congress, nor even a general in the army. I am only a government clerk."

" 'I greet you again, Mr. Flag-Maker,' replied the gay voice. 'I know you well. You are the man who worked in the swelter of yesterday straightening out the tangle of that farmer's homestead in Idaho, or perhaps you found the mistake in that Indian contract in Oklahoma, or helped to clear that patent for opening of that new ditch in Colorado, or made that mine in Illinois more safe, or brought relief to the old soldier in Wyoming. No matter; whichever one of these beneficent individuals you may be, I give you greetings, Mr. Flag-Maker.'

"I was about to pass on, when the Flag stopped me with these words:

"Yesterday the President spoke a word that made happier the future of 10,000,000 peons in Mexico, but that act looms no larger on the flag than the struggle which the boy in Georgia is making to win the corn club prize this summer.'

" 'Yesterday the President spoke a word that made open the door of Alaska, but a mother in Michigan worked from sunrise until far into the night to give her boy an education. She, too, is making the flag.'

"Then came a great shout from the flag: 'The work

The Makers of the Flag

that we do is the making of the flag. I am not the flag; not at all. I am but its shadow. I am whatever you make me; nothing more. I am your belief in yourself, your dream of what a people may become. I live in changing life, a life of moods and passions, of heartbreaks and tired muscles.'

" 'Sometimes I am strong with pride, when men do an honest work, fitting the rails together truly.'

" 'Sometimes I droop, for then purpose has gone from me, and cynically I play the coward.'

" 'Sometimes I am loud, garish, and full of that ego that blasts judgment.'

" 'But always I am all that you hope to be, and have the courage to try for.'

" 'I am the day's work for the weakest man and the largest dream of the most daring.'

" 'I am song and fear, struggle, panic and hope.'

" 'I am the Constitution and the courts, statutes and the statute-makers, soldier and dreadnaught, drayman and street sweep, cook, counselor and clerk.'

" 'I am the battle of yesterday and the mistake of to-morrow.'

" 'I am the mystery of the men who do without knowing why.'

" 'I am the clutch of an idea and the reasoned purpose of resolution.'

" 'I am no more than what you believe me to be, and I am all that you believe I can be.'

" 'I am what you make me, nothing more.'

" 'I swing before your eyes as a bright gleam of color, a symbol of yourself, the pictured suggestion of that big thing which makes this nation. My stars and stripes are your dream and your labors. They are bright with cheer, brilliant with courage, firm with faith, because you have made them so out of your hearts. For you are the makers of the flag, and it is well that you glory in the making.' "

The Day I Belonged to the Flag

by The Late President Dwight D. Eisenhower

"My first day at West Point, June 14, 1911 had been rough. My class mates and I had been barked at and ordered by upperclassmen to do all sorts of ridiculous chores, on the double. All 285 of us were weary and resentful. Towards evening, however, we assembled outdoors with the American flag floating majestically above us as we were sworn in as Cadets of the United States Military Academy.

"It was an impressive ceremony, and as I looked up at the National Colors and swore my allegiance, I realized promptly that now I BELONGED TO THE FLAG.

"It is a moment I have never forgotten. Later I became Color Sergeant of our class and my final year at West Point it was my privilege to carry the American Flag at all official parades and ceremonies.

"No honor could have meant more to me. To tell you why I love and respect our flag so much would take a book for it would be a long day's story of America. Briefly, I love our flag because it is the most beautiful National banner of all and because it stands today as always for the finest nation on earth.

"Today we urgently need a new commitment to the basic principles that made our nation great. Our flag is a symbol of these principles and I would hope that all of us might find some way to display it not merely on patriotic holidays but every day in the year. Such a visible upsurge of respect for the flag and country will do much to bring about a new National solidarity, a renewed pride and faith in America."

Copyright, Dwight D. Eisenhower, 1969—used by permission of Doubleday & Co., Inc.

Quotes by Famous Americans

Rev. Henry Ward Beecher (1813–1887) *"In 1777, within a few days of one year after the Declaration of Independence, the congress of the colonies in the confederate states assembled and ordained this glorious national flag which we now hold and defend, and advanced it full high before God and all men as the flag of liberty. It was no holiday flag gorgeously emblazoned for gaiety or vanity. It was a solemn national symbol. Our flag carried American ideas, American history, and American feelings. Beginning with the colonies and coming down to our time, in its sacred heraldry, in its glorious insignia, it has gathered and stored chiefly this supreme idea; DIVINE RIGHT OF LIBERTY IN MEN. Every color means liberty; every thread means liberty; every form of star or beam or stripe of light means liberty; not lawlessness, not license; but organized, institutional liberty—liberty through law, and laws for liberty! Accept it, then, in all its fullness of meaning. It is not a painted rag. It is a whole national history. It is the Constitution. It is the Government. It is the free people that stand in the Government on the Constitution. Forget not what it means; and for the sake of its ideas, be true to your country's flag."*

Francis Bellamy (1855–1931) who wrote the Pledge of Allegiance to the Flag, said in 1930, just before he died in Tampa, Florida:—*"It has been repeated by generations of new voices, not only in every public school in the nation, but by organizations of men and women who have used this familiar formula to express their patriotic sentiment, until at last it has been called by some enthusiasts the National Creed. ... I have the happiness of realizing that I once, in my young manhood, contributed to my Country an easily remembered symbol of patriotism which has*

Quotes By Famous Americans

become historic and has been in many millions of individuals a spur to their love of Country and Flag."

Wallace F. Bennett, United States Senator from Utah, said in a letter to the author Oct. 30, 1970:

"I love the American Flag because it stands for everything that has made this country the greatest nation on earth. It has always been a standard of liberty and a torch of freedom to oppressed peoples throughout the world. Today this nation is beset with many problems. There are those among us and those among our critics abroad who prophesy the end of America as we now know it. However, although America does face great challenges and problems today, the ideals and principles symbolized by the flag will yet carry us through. The flag at one and the same time is large enough to encompass the diverse segments of our society, yet small enough to signify the unity of all patriotic Americans. So long as the love of liberty continues to burn in the hearts of mankind, the American flag will stand as a symbol of man's best hope on this good earth."

Paul Fannin, United States Senator from Arizona, on Sept. 22, 1970, in a letter to the author, said:

"Have you wondered why the anarchists and demonstrators concentrate their attacks on the flag, pulling it down, defiling it, burning it?

"Apologists for these destroyers would have us believe they are motivated by high ideals and a noble desire to reform our social, governmental and financial institutions. The truth is, their objective is not reform, but total destruction. Those who tear down the flag reveal their hatred for everything good and great in our country, because the flag is a symbol of what we want America to be—a land of justice, opportunity, equality and compassion."

Quotes By Famous Americans

Dante B. Fascell, Member of Congress from Florida, in a letter to the author August 11, 1970, said:—
"The Flag is a symbol of our great American Heritage, a heritage of freedom; freedom bravely fought for and bravely gained. It is a flag that is large enough to unfurl and spread its protection over all of America and all of her citizens. It stands for and shelters all people. The Flag is the property of all Americans. Its care is entrusted to all the people, never just to a self-elected elite who wish to propagate its reverence to the exclusion of others, promoting disunion in the name of patriotism and debasing the Flag by encouraging its use as a symbol of one faction or another. The Flag knows of no faction other than liberty, which is why it should be honored. Cherish liberty or cherish the Flag; you uphold both when you uphold the other."

Ulysses S. Grant (1822–1885), 18th President of the United States. *"There is no name so great that it should be placed upon the flag of our country."*

Benjamin Harrison (1833–1901), 23rd President of the United States. *"I, Benjamin Harrison, President of the United States of America do hereby appoint Friday, October 21, 1892, the four hundredth anniversary of the Discovery of America by Columbus, as a general holiday for the people of the United States. . . . Let the National Flag float over every school house in the country, and the exercises be such as shall impress upon our youth the patriotic duties of American citizenship."*

Samuel Myer Issacs (1804–1878), publisher of the JEWISH MESSENGER, wrote in 1861:
"Stand by the flag! The time is past for forbearance and temporizing. We are now to act . . . to rally as one may for the Union and the Constitution . . .

Quotes By Famous Americans

which extends its hearty invitation to all the oppressed of all nations . . . and guaranteeing to all, the free exercise of their religious opinions, extending to all, liberty, justice and equality . . . Then stand by your flag! . . . Whether native or Israelite, stand by it, and you are doing your duty, and acting well your part on the side of liberty and justice."

John V. Lindsay, Mayor of New York City, in an address to the National Guard Association, September 14, 1970, said:

"Our nation shares common principles. It desperately needs a shared symbol of our unity. And that's what the flag stands for.

"It stands for the promise of American life—for economic security and decent jobs, for more schools and housing and better health care and justice.

"The flag stands for the right to believe what you want and speak as you must. Its design conveys its real meaning. There wouldn't be individual stars and individual stripes if we were all supposed to think the same and act the same and support the same policies. There are thirteen stripes—and fifty stars —and two hundred million Americans, all free men and women.

"The flag ultimately stands for service to our country. This is our country, right or wrong. But if we care about it, we must work to make it right. As we work, conscience and intellect may sometimes lead us to differ, one from another. But the same flag must still fly over all of us—at baseball games and peace rallies—in this hall and at a rock festival. It is the sign of a duty that transcends our differences—a duty to serve that binds us together in the common enterprise we call America.

"That's what the flag stands for. For our dreams and our hopes, our ideals and our principles. We must defend it. Against others, if they threaten it.

Quotes By Famous Americans

Against ourselves, if we degrade it.

There is a lot to argue about today and a lot to fight for. But it is wrong to reduce the flag to a partisan political signal or a debating point. And it is wrong to defile it in order to provoke citizens.

"For beyond the names, epithets, despite our disputes and our divisions, we all live under the American flag. Let us serve it—and each other."

Major Gen. Arthur MacArthur (1845–1912), served in the United States Army for 47 years. *"The flag of the American Union is a visible symbol of the ideal aspirations of the American people. It is the one focus in which all unite in reverential devotion. We differ in religion; we differ in politics; we engage in violent disputes as to the true meaning of the Constitution, and even challenge the wisdom of some of its provisions; we inject self-interest and cupidity into most of the ordinary transactions of daily life, but through the sanctifying folds of the flag the collective intelligence of the Nation rises superior to the wisdom of any of its parts, and thus ensures the perpetuity of the Republic."*

George McGovern, United States Senator from South Dakota, stated on August 26, 1970:

"I believe that the flag should be held high above the debate . . . We have sincere differences . . . But I believe that this nation will endure and prosper and that we can all maintain our pride in many of its accomplishments and in its great potential. We shall want to preserve the strong sentiments all Americans have for their flag, keeping it out of partisan politics so that we may all rally 'round it again."

Edmund S. Muskie, United States Senator from Maine: *"To me, the American flag will always symbolize the basic freedoms guaranteed all Americans by our Constitution and our heritage. The flag means*

Quotes By Famous Americans

freedom of religion. It means freedom of speech. It means that wherever the flag flies, there are men who believe in the concept of inalienable rights. Those who would make our flag a partisan banner, fail to perceive its significance. The American flag flies neither for the left nor the right. It has no party. It has no ideology save that of the Constitution itself. As long as men pursue the goal of freedom, it will be honored and cherished."

Richard M. Nixon, President of the United States, said on Nov. 25, 1970:
"Woodrow Wilson, speaking at Independence Hall in 1914, expressed the feeling that I deeply share, and that I know most Americans share with me, when he said that 'a patriotic American . . . is never so proud of the great flag under which he lives as when it comes to mean to other people as well as to himself a symbol of hope and liberty.'"

O. Henry (William Sydney Porter) (1862–1919), noted author. *"You can't appreciate home till you've left it, money till it's spent, your wife till she's joined a woman's club, nor Old Glory till you see it hanging on a broomstick on a shanty of a consul in a foreign town."*

General Horace Porter (1837–1921), Ambassador to France. *"I want to see the young men of this land taught that our banner should be to them like the banner in the sky which appeared to Constantine of old, which turned him back into the path of duty from which he had strayed. It should be taught that it is to be their pillar of cloud by day; their pillar of fire by night; that it is to wave about them in victory, be their rallying point in defeat, and if they offer up their lives a sacrifice in its defense, its gently folds will rest upon their bosoms in death."*

Quotes By Famous Americans

Edna Dean Proctor (1829–1923), author and poet. *"Invincible banner! The flag of the free, Oh, where treads the foot that would falter for Thee?"*

Herbert R. Rainwater, Commander-in-Chief of The Veterans of Foreign Wars of The United States— 1970–71, said on August 18, 1970 in Miami, Florida:

"When I look at the American Flag I see more than a beautiful banner. And I see more than a symbol of freedom, justice and equality. The Stars and Stripes stands for those values as no other symbol can.

But our Flag also represents enduring strength— the ability of a nation and its people to overcome adversity and, in the process, become more viable.

I look at our Flag and I see Bunker Hill and Gettysburg. I see the burning of Washington, the sinking of the Maine, the battle of the Marne, Pearl Harbor, Kasserine Pass, Bastogne, Pusan and the seige of Khe Sanh. I see the Depression and the Dust Bowl. And, yes, I see trouble in cities and disorder on campuses.

But that Flag of the United States remains indestructible. So do all of the fine things it represents. The Stars and Stripes will ride the breeze tomorrow, and for a thousand tomorrows if we so will. AND WE DO SO WILL."

Admiral H. G. Rickover, father of the Navy's nuclear ship propulsion program, said after the first sea trials of the U.S.S. Francis Scott Key, nuclear submarine, Dec. 3rd, 1966:—

"Francis Scott Key caught the mystique the flag has for us, who are a nation not only by consanguinity, not by a long common history, but by devotion to an abstract concept the concept of liberty under law. Dennis W. Brogan . . . once tried to explain . . . what the flag means to Americans. 'It is more,' he

Quotes By Famous Americans

said, 'than a mere symbol . . . it is the regimental color of a regiment in which all Americans are enrolled.' "

Charles Sumner (1811–1874) *"There is the National Flag. We must be cold, indeed, who can look upon its folds rippling in the breeze without pride of country. If in a foreign land, the flag is companionship, and country itself, with all its endearments."*

Lawrence Phelps Tower, President of the U.S. Flag Foundation at 115 E. 86th St., New York City, N.Y. said;—*"Throughout the history of mankind, symbols have exerted an impelling influence upon the lives of men. The Cross, The Flag are the embodiment of our ideals, and teach us not only how to live, but how to die."*

Dr. Kenneth D. Wells, President-Emeritus, Freedom's Foundation, Valley Forge, Pa., said on May 30, 1968:—*"Our American flag is the dramatic, visual symbol of the unity of our country and the liberty under law. It represents duty, honor, and country. Men of every color, creed and race have given their lives to protect the free way of life for which it stands and will continue to pay any price to keep the flag flying, representing American aspirations of bravery, faith and purity."*

Woodrow (Thomas) Wilson (1856–1924), 28th President of the United States. *"We look to the noisy places, where partisans are expressing passion; instead of trying to attune our ears to that voiceless mass of men who merely go about their daily tasks, try to be honorable, try to serve the people they love, try to live worthy of the great communities to which they belong. These are the breath of the nation's nostrils; these are the sinew of its might. There are*

Quotes By Famous Americans

no days of special patriotism. There are no days when you should be more patriotic than on other days, and I ask you to wear every day in your heart our Flag of the Union."

Robert C. Winthrop (1809–1894), U.S. Senator from Massachusetts. *"Our flag is our national ensign, pure and simple, behold it! Listen to it! Every star has a tongue, every stripe is articulate."*

Remember Me?

Hello—remember me? I'm your flag. Some folks call me Old Glory, others call me the Stars and Stripes, the Ensign, or just . . . the flag. But whatever they call me, I am your flag. And, as I proudly state, The Flag of the United States of America.

Something has been bothering me lately. I was wondering if I might talk it over with you. It's about you and me.

I remember sometime ago (I think it was Memorial Day, or was it the 4th of July) when people lined up on both sides of the street to watch a parade. When your father saw me coming along, waving in the breeze, he took his hat off and held it against his left shoulder. His hand was directly over his heart. Remember?

And you. I remember you! Standing there—straight as a soldier. You didn't have a hat on, but you gave the correct salute. They taught you in school to place your hand over your heart. Remember your little Sister? Not to be outdone, she was saluting the same as you. I was proud, very proud, as I came down that street. Oh, Yes, there were some Servicemen there, standing at attention, giving the salute. Ladies as well as men, civilians as well as military, paid me respect . . . reverence.

Now, if I sound a bit conceited . . . well . . . I have a right to. I represent the finest country in the world —The United States of America. More than one aggressive nation has tried to haul me down, only to feel the fury of this freedom loving country. Many of you had to go overseas to defend me. A lot more blood has been shed since those patriotic parades of long ago and I've had a few stars added since you were a boy, but I'm still the same old flag.

Dad is gone now . . . and the hometown has a new look. The last time I came down your street, I noticed that some of the old landmarks had given way to a number of new buildings and homes. Yessir, the old

Remember Me?

town sure has changed. I guess I have too, 'cause I don't feel as proud as I did back then.

I see youngsters running and shouting through the streets, college boys and girls disrupting our campuses, people selling hot dogs and beer while our National Anthem is played . . . everything from apathy to riots. They don't seem to know—or care—who I am. Not too long ago, I saw a man take his hat off when I came by . . . he looked around, didn't see anybody else with theirs off . . . so he quickly put his back on.

Now—when I come down your street, you just stand there with your hands in your pockets. Occasionally, you give me a small glance and then look away. When I think of all the places I've been . . . Normandy, Guadalcanal; Iwo Jima; Battle of the Bulge; Korea; and now, Vietnam; I wonder—what's happened? I'm still the same old flag.

How can I be expected to fly high and proud from buildings and homes when within them, there is no thought, love, or respect for me? Whatever happened to patriotism? Your patriotism? Have you forgotten what I stand for? Have you forgotten all the battlefields where men fought and died to keep this nation free? When you salute me, you salute them. Take a look at the Memorial Honor Rolls sometime. Look at the names of those who never came back. Some of them were friends or relatives of yours . . . maybe even went to school with you. That's what you're saluting—NOT ME!

Well, it won't be long before I come down your street again. So, when you see me, stand straight, and place your hand over your heart. Do this because I represent you. You'll see me wave back, my salute to you . . .

Copyright 1970 by David C. Graham, Box 11247, San Diego, CA 92111. Reprinted by permission. 9 12 copies suitable for framing—$1.

What the Flag Means to Me

"The band had started to play and all 70,000 people in the stadium rose to their feet except one. They stood reverently at attention while Old Glory was raised to the highest pole. The only one who wasn't standing was a young boy.

"I heard the man with him say, 'Why didn't you stand up when the flag was raised? Don't you know that when the flag is raised, you aren't supposed to slouch? Don't you know that thousands of brave men have fought and died for that bit of red, white and blue?'

"The boy couldn't seem to come up with an answer.

'Son,' he said, 'let me tell you something about our flag that I hope you will never forget. That flag flew proudly at Bunker Hill. It flapped softly in the cold winter air at Valley Forge and on a dozen battlefields of the Revolution. The ragged Continentals saluted it proudly as they paraded by it after the great victory at Yorktown.'

" 'It whipped sharply in the breeze from the topmasts of our frigates in 1812. Some years later dusty cavalrymen carried it proudly through Texas and into Mexico during the Mexican War.'

" 'A hundred years ago it flew through all the bloody battles of the Civil War, from Bull Run to Manassas, Chancellorsville to Vicksburg, Antietam and Gettysburg. At Appomatox it was fondly raised by the victorious soldiers of the Federal Army.'

" 'In Cuba and at the Battle of Manila in the Philippines during the Spanish-American War our soldiers and sailors thrilled at its sight.'

" 'Then, during the First World War, it saw a thousand battles in the muddy trenches in France.'

" 'More recently, from 1941 to 1945, that flag was landed at Africa, Italy, Normandy and on a thousand sweating islands in the Pacific. You remember that great moment when the Marines planted it on Iwo Jima?'

What the Flag Means to Me

" 'Then came Korea, and once again the sight of that flag brought tears to the eyes of many brave men.'

" 'So, whenever you see the flag, I just hope you remember the blood, sweat and tears that men have gone through to keep our beloved country free.'

"The boy looked up at the man. 'You bet I'll remember next time, Dad,' I said."

(This is the winning essay in a contest sponsored by the Darling Whitney Chapter of the Daughters of the American Revolution in Port Washington, New York, in 1961. It was written by John Stewart Snibbe, 14 years old, who was killed in an auto accident in 1969.)

"The American flag means to me, my home, my parents, my relatives and lots more. The flag means freedom for you and me. Being able to do what we want as long as it doesn't hurt others and being able to live where we want. In America you have a choice to vote for any candidate you want, and any person rich or poor can run for office for which they are qualified."
By Pamela Ginsberg.

"**F** stands for Freedom, on land and on sea,
    for America is the land for me.
 L stands for Liberty, for love and for care,
    look at America, you'll find it there!
 A stands for Achievement, America too,
    American achievement is the best thing for you.
 G stands for Greatness, Glory, and all that is Good.
    if you don't love the flag, you certainly should.
F-L-A-G is America's symbol, land of the free,
And that is what our flag means to me!"
By Stuart Knox Chapin.

(The above essays were written by two ten-year olds in the Fifth Grade of Rockway Elementary School, Miami, Florida, in September, 1970).

What the Pledge of Allegiance Means to New Citizens

On Tuesday, June 2, 1970, in Miami, Florida, nine hundred and one persons became United States citizens. It was a mass ceremony and on the bench sat Judge Ted Cabot and Judge Edward S. Klein of the Civil Court.

Jean Wardlow, a Staff Writer for the Miami Herald, covered the story and this is what she wrote. The story appeared on June 3. (Permission was granted by George Beebe, Senior Managing Editor, and Larry Jinks, Managing Editor of the Miami Herald (A Knight Newspaper) to reprint this article.)

"I pledge allegiance ..."

You might wonder about the time they chose—the campus voices still echoing; others sounding yet from ghettos, grape fields, auto factories, Wall Street, chambers of political men.

"... to the flag of the United States of America ..."

While a nation bends and sways with dissent and assent and new voices of many ages come from many sides, they picked this time to tie themselves to that country. More than one called it "The Greatest Country." And they said it with surprise in their voices, that anyone could doubt it.

"... and to the Republic for which it stands ..."

Nine hundred and one asked to become U.S. Citizens Tuesday; 871 could come ... It was a mass ceremony of becoming a U.S. Citizen ("first, this group on the right, please stand, raise your right hand and repeat after me ..."), and the federal court this day was a lighted stage draped with burgundy-red velvet and cream-colored curtains with the blue-covered desk in the center, it was, after all, red, white and blue.

"... one Nation under God ..."

What the Pledge Allegiance Means to New Citizens

Why had they chosen this time? A tall, Canadian-born Robert Scruton, 22, said this:—"After three years of fighting for this country, I thought it was the thing to do." He had served in Vietnam.

"... *indivisible* ..."

Charles E. Anderson, in his USARSO uniform ... He came a long way to do it ... from Panama.

"... *with liberty* ..."

"This country opened its heart to us when we needed a home," said a Cuban who didn't want his name used because of family members still on the island. "It gave us a new chance. Now I want to do what I can for it."

He was a gray-haired man; a time in life, perhaps, when others would think of less responsibilities, rather than assuming new ones.

"When you have lost freedom, then you appreciate it like a rare jewel," he said.

Into assigned seats they filtered—Olga Martinez ... Moses Stein ... Antonia Romas ... Marie Fortunato ...

"... *and justice* ..."

And then two judges spoke to them: Judge Cabot's remarks—"It is through the infusion of new citizens that the strength and high vitality of this country can be maintained." And Judge Klein told them that, "as a son of an immigrant that occasion has particular significance." His mother came from Russia in 1905.

Nine hundred people took this time to tie themselves to a new country. The echoes they heard were not from recent cries. Perhaps they were from words of history and promise and a certain line in the pledge they made. It was a line with meaning:

"... *for all.*"

Unusual Places the Flag Was Carried

1787—Captain Robert Gray (1755–1806) was the first man who carried the Star-Spangled Banner around the world on his sailing vessel.

Gray set out from Boston in 1787 to trade in furs between northwestern America and China. He sailed around the tip of South America and went on to China. He returned to Boston in 1790. He again set out in 1792 to search for rivers on the West Coast that might carry him across the country. He discovered the mouth of a great river and named it the Columbia River after his ship Columbia.

His discovery was later a basis for the United States' claim to the Oregon territory. He sailed for over 42,000 miles. It took him three years to circle the globe.

1806—Zebulon Montgomery Pike (1779–1813) soldier and early explorer of the West, discovered the highest peak of the Rocky Mountains in Colorado. It was named Pike's Peak after him but he never got to the top.

1820—Major Stephen Harriman Long (1784–1864) finally made it to the top of Pike's Peak and planted the flag on the summit. The flag then had 23 stars. In 1905 a huge searchlight was placed on top of Pike's Peak. One of the highest meteorological stations in the world is maintained by the United States Weather Bureau on the Peak.

1898—Old Glory on San Juan Hill, Cuba, during the Spanish-American War. In J. W. Bennett's book, "Roosevelt and the Republic," written in 1906 he wrote, "Lieutenant Preston of the Sixteenth Regiment, whose trumpeter sounded the charge, brings up the national and regimental colors, and they wave over the fort. Col. Theodore Roosevelt and his Rough Riders of five hundred men, loomed in the news and

Unusual Places Where the Flag Was Carried

"slouch" hats and brown duck uniforms of the Rough Riders ran a close second in popularity to Old Glory itself..."

Unusual Places the Flag Was Carried

by National Geographic Society Expeditions

1912—Professor Robert F. Griggs (1881–1962) on an expedition sponsored by the National Geographic Society took the Society's flag topped by the American flag, to Mount Katmai region of Alaska, June, 1912, to study a volcanic explosion and the subsequent ash-fall which buried an area as large as Connecticut.

1928—Richard E. Byrd's (1888–1957) explorations by air won him fame as "Admiral of the Ends of the Earth." Commander Byrd was the first man to fly over both the North and South Poles. With Floyd Bennett (1890–1928) as his pilot and mechanic he flew over the North Pole in 1926. In 1928 Byrd organized a scientific expedition to the Antarctic. His second expedition was in 1933–35, the third in 1939–40, and a fourth in 1947. The 1928 trip was sponsored jointly by the National Geographic Society and the U.S. Navy. When Byrd flew over the Antarctic he dropped the American flag weighted with a stone from Floyd Bennett's grave. Byrd wrote four books about his explorations.

1934—Charles William Beebe (1877–1962) in August, 1934, carried the Society's flag, topped by Old Glory, attached to the cable on his bathysphere, down to a record dive of 3,028 feet, eight miles off Bermuda. Otis Barton, a scientist, accompanied him.

Unusual Places Where the Flag Was Carried

1963—Barry C. Bishop, one of National Geographic Society's staff men carried the Society's flag, topped by Old Glory, to the top of Mount Everest, the earth's highest point, 29,028 ft., May 22, 1963. This was the National Geographic Society's American-Mt. Everest Expedition, which scaled the South Col and the West Ridge.

(National Geographic Society Expeditions have carried the flag to too many unusual places to mention them all.)

The Flag at the North Pole

On April 6th, 1909, Robert E. Peary became the first man to reach the North Pole. With four Eskimos, Ooqueah, Ootah, Egingwah, Seegloo and with Matthew A. Henson, his Negro assistant, (who had worked with Peary since 1887) he photographed his team at the top of the world. An American flag flew from an ice cap in the background.

In 1898, Peary's wife Josephine, "the constant aid and inspiration of my life," made him a flag with 45 stars. Peary carried it wrapped around his body. He deposited five pieces of this flag in five different places along his trails in search for the Pole. Thus he actually desecrated the flag but was never censored for it.

A corner piece of the flag was placed in a bottle at Cape Morris Jesup in 1900, and was found by Donald Baxter MacMillan, another American Polar explorer, in May, 1909, who left it there.

A triangle of the flag was put in the ice at 87°06′ in April, 1906, and this piece was never found. Another rectangle of the flag was left at Cape Columbia, June 1906, and found by scientists in 1953. A small piece, cut from the top center of the flag, was marked Cape Thomas Hubbard and left there in June, 1906. MacMillan found this piece in 1914.

Peary cut a diagonal band from the flag and deposited it at the North Pole, but it was never found. Peary wrote on a note placed in a bottle with this piece of the flag, "90° N. Lat., North Pole, April 6, 1909. I have today hoisted the National Ensign of the United States of America at this place which my observations indicate to be the North Polar axis of the earth..."

Peary died in 1920. His wife presented the pieced-together flag to the National Geographic Society where it is on display in the Society's Explorer's Hall on 17th Street in Washington D.C. Peary served as President of this Society from 1901 to 1906.

The Flag around the World Underwater

Captain Edward L. Beach, Jr., USN, wrote a book about his experiences as Commander of the Triton, called "Around the World Submerged—the Voyage of the Triton." The Triton, a 447-foot nuclear-powered submarine was commissioned on Nov. 10, 1959. Vice-Admiral H. G. Rickover, USN, made the Triton possible. Captain Beach called him "One of the great men of our time."

Captain Beach also wrote a book called "The Wreck of the Memphis," which tells of the wreck of one of the largest battle cruisers ever built by the United States Navy. It was captained by his father, Captain Edward L. Beach, Sr. In August, 1916 the Memphis was wrecked by a tidal wave off the coast of Santo Domingo. For this Captain Beach's father was court-martialed, but later exonerated. The flag from the Memphis was saved by a member of the Memphis crew, Stanley P. Moran, who gave it to young Captain Beach.

The voyage of the Triton followed Magellan's route around the world and traveled submerged more than 36,000 nautical miles. In Captain Beach's cabin was the flag which had been on his father's ill-fated ship, forty-four years before.

On Tuesday, May 10th, 1960, the Triton surfaced at New London, Conn., 83 days after the epic trip began.

Flying from the highest periscope was the rather old and slightly weather-beaten flag that had flown on his father's ship the Memphis in 1916.

He wrote, "As I glanced about me, a gust of wind caught Father's old flag, flying from the top of our extended periscope, and straightened its ancient folds in reminiscent glory."

Captain Beach was flown to the White House after the Triton docked, and there President Eisenhower cited him for extraordinary heroism and conspicuous gallantry. This trip will go down in history as one of the great adventures of the sea.

The U.S.S. Francis Scott Key

The ceremony of christening the U.S.S. Francis Scott Key, the nuclear submarine (SSBN 657) took place on April 23, 1966, at Groton, Connecticut.

Two direct descendants of Francis Scott Key, Edith Claude Jarvis and her cousin Marjory Key Thorne, christened the submarine.

At the time of the commissioning Edith Jarvis presented a copy of "Birth of the Star-Spangled Banner Anthem," an original painting in the Peale Museum in Baltimore, Md., to be hung in the wardroom of the submarine.

The commissioning flag given to Mrs. Jarvis, was presented by her to the Flag House in Baltimore. The Flag House was built in 1793. Mary Pickersgill lived there from 1807 until her death in 1857. She made the "Star-Spangled Banner" that Francis Scott Key saw "by the dawn's early light" flying over Fort McHenry, and which inspired Mrs. Jarvis' ancestor to write our National Anthem.

This flag was the only American flag ever to have more than 13 stripes. Its design of 15 stars and 15 stripes was proposed in Congress and was the second Flag Act passed by our Congress on January 13, 1794.

Mrs. Jarvis is an interested member of the Flag House Association which maintains Mary Pickersgill's historic home which is now a museum.

Mrs. Jarvis is also a member of the Society of Sponsors of the United States Navy and one of their Board of Trustees. This society is comprised of ladies who have christened ships of our Navy and they come from all over the United States. Each Spring they meet in Washington for three days. One of their aims is the granting of scholarships to qualified boys who are preparing to take the U.S. Naval Academy examinations.

The Flag Flies on the Moon

On Monday, July 20, 1969 man took his first step on the moon. Apollo 11 carried three men, Edwin E. (Buzz) Aldrin, Jr., Michael Collins and Neil Armstrong, who made the greatest voyage in human history.

Neil Armstrong was the first man to set foot on the moon. Then Aldrin climbed down the nine-rung ladder and joined Armstrong on the lunar surface. They carried out their scheduled work, then set up an American flag. Because there is no wind on the moon and the flag would not be able to wave, it was fixed carefully to a grid of anodized aluminum bracing.

Flags of 136 nations and 50 states and the District of Columbia made the trip to the moon, and three cotton flags will remain inside the module. They are the United States flag, the flags of the House of Representatives and the Senate and the flag of the United Nations.

Dr. Thomas O. Paine, chief of the civilian space agency, when asked if an American flag or a United Nations flag was going to be planted on the moon, said:

"We looked at this question very carefully and concluded that the planting of the American flag is the appropriate action. This mighty enterprise has essentially been carried out by hundreds of thousands of Americans and funded by the American taxpayer, although many other nations have contributed.

"Although we all recognize that our Apollo program is built on technology and science from around the world—not only in this generation but in all previous generations—still it's an American program, and we are proud and pleased to have the privilege of unfurling our American flag there; not to take possession of the moon for America but to recognize our nation's achievement."

The Flag Flies on the Moon

The Third Flag on the Moon

Apollo 14 lifted off from Cape Kennedy on January 31st, 1971 at 4:03 p.m.

The three astronauts were Capt. Alan B. Shepherd Jr., Comdr. Edgar D. Mitchell of the Navy and Comdr. Stuart A. Roosa of the Air Force.

After a journey of more than a quarter of a million miles, they landed on the moon in the Fra Mauro Highlands, in the landing craft Antares, while the command ship Kitty Hawk, piloted by Comdr. Stuart A. Roosa circled in lunar orbit for 33½ hours.

The astronuats were beset by many delays. The large umbrella-shaped, S-band antenna, used to beam signals to earth, refused to open properly. It took nearly ten minutes to erect the third U.S. Flag on the moon.

The three astronauts splashed down in the Pacific Ocean Feb. 9th at 4:04 p.m. The U.S.S. New Orleans recovered the astronauts and their command ship.

The Fourth Flag on the Moon

Apollo 15 lifted off July 26th, 1971. The astronauts on this historic journey were: David R. Scott, James B. Irwin and Alfred M. Worden.

July 31st, Commander David Scott and James Irwin landed on the moon and Scott photographed Irwin saluting the American Flag, which they had just set up.

When the astronauts stepped on the deck of the recovery ship, the U.S. Carrier Okinawa, and ended their 295-hour, 12-minute flight, the flight controllers in Houston, Texas broke out small American Flags and cheered.

There were many firsts for the Apollo 15 flight. It was the first use of a moon car which carried Scott and Irwin 17.4 miles along the foothills of the Hadley-Rille Apennine Mountains; the first "walk" outside a spacecraft in deep space; first launching of a satellite in moon orbit and first look out the top of a lunar module to survey a landing site.

The Flag on Postage Stamps

It is estimated that there are more than 25,000,000 stamp collectors in the world. Stamps with our Star-Spangled Banner are sought after by stamp collectors. The first such stamp was issued in 1869.

1869–80—Shield, Eagle and Flags. 30 cent stamp.

1898—"Fremont on the Rocky Mountains" depicting him planting the U.S. flag on a mountain summit. 5 cent stamp.

1903—Washington portrait flanked by two U.S. flags. 2 cent stamp.

1909—"Fulton's Steamship **Clermont**" which is flying the U.S. flag. 2 cent stamp.

1919—"Victory and Flags" depicting U.S. flag and those of WW 1 Allies. 3 cent stamp.

1931—Pulaski portrait flanked by U.S. and Polish flags. 2 cent stamp.

1933—Washington's headquarters at Newburgh, New York showing U.S. flag flying. 3 cent stamp.

1935—Michigan State Seal flanked by U.S. and Michigan flags. 3 cent stamp.

1936—Navy Issue with ships flying U.S. flag. 1 cent, 2 cents and 3 cent stamps.

1944—"Golden Spike Ceremony" with U.S. flag in foreground. 3 cent stamp.

1944—"Savannah" flying U.S. flag. 3 cent stamp.

1945—"Roosevelt and White House" showing U.S. flag flying from atop the White House. 3 cent stamp.

1945—Texas Statehood Issue. To commemorate the 100th Anniversary of the admission of Texas to Statehood. Shows flags of the United States and the State of Texas. 3 cent stamp.

1946—"Capture of Santa Fe" with U.S. flag flying from pole. 3 cent stamp.

1947—"Constitution" with U.S. flag. 3 cent stamp.

1948—Francis Scott Key. 1814 & 1948. 3 cent stamp.

1950—"National Capital Sesquicentennial" issue showing U.S. flag flying from atop the buildings. 3 cent stamp.

The Flag on Postage Stamps

1952—Betsy Ross Issue. Shows Betsy Ross showing flag to Gen. George Washington, Robert Morris and George Ross. 200th anniversary of the birth of Betsy Ross, maker of the first American Flag. 3 cent stamp.

1952—Lafayette Issue. To commemorate the 175th anniversary of the arrival of Marquis de Lafayette in America. Shows flags of U.S. and France. 3 cent stamp.

1957—Flag Issue, "Old Glory" (48 stars). This was first issue where artist's name was given. Designed by Victor S. McCloskey, Jr. 4 cent stamp.

1958—"Lincoln and Stephen A. Douglas Debating" showing U.S. Flag in background. 4 cent stamp.

1959—49 Star Flag Issue. Designed by Stevan Dohanos. 4 cent stamp.

1960—50 Star Flag Issue. Also by Stevan Dohanos.

1962—Girl Scouts Issue. To commemorate the 50th Anniversary of the Girl Scouts of America. Shows Senior Girl Scout and flag. Designed by Ward Brackett. 4 cent stamp.

1963—Flag Issue. Shows Flag over White House, designed by Robert J. Jones. 5 cent stamp.

1964—Register and Vote Issue. To publicize the campaign to draw more voters to the polls. Designed by Victor S. McCloskey, Jr. 5 cent stamp.

1965—Battle of New Orleans Issue. To commemorate the sesquicentennial of the Battle of New Orleans, Chalmette Plantation, Jan. 8, 1815, which established 150 years of peace and friendship between the United States and Great Britain. Shows General Andrew Jackson, the flag and Sesquicentennial Medal. Designed by Robert J. Jones. 5 cent stamp.

1966—Savings Bond–Serviceman Issue. Shows Statue of Liberty and "Old Glory" with the legend "We appreciate our Servicemen." Designed by Stevan Dohanos (photograph by Bob Noble) 5 cent stamp.

1967—"Space-Twins" showing U.S. flag on suit of

The Flag on Postage Stamps

astronaut. 5 cent stamp.
1968—Flag issue. Shows flag and White House. Designed by Stevan Dohanos. 5 cent stamp.
1968—July 4th—Historic Flag Series. Issued to show flags carried by American colonists and citizens of the new United States.

    (1) Fort Moultrie Flag, 1776
    (2) Fort McHenry Flag, 1795–1818
    (3) Washington's Cruisers Flag, 1775
    (4) Bennington Flag 1777
    (5) Rhode Island Flag 1775
    (6) First Stars and Stripes 1777
    (7) Bunker Hill Flag 1775
    (8) Grand Union Flag 1776
    (9) Philadelphia Light Horse Flag 1775
  (10) First Navy Jack 1775

1969—Grandma Moses "July Fourth" showing U.S. flag on pole. 6 cent stamp.
1969—Eisenhower with U.S. flag in background. 6 cent stamp.
1970—"Woman Suffrage" with U.S. flag in background. 6 cent stamp.
1970—Great Northwest–Fort Snelling Commemorative issue. Shows Fort Snelling which was built on the banks of the Minneapolis River in Mendota, Minnesota, in 1820. Designed by David K. Stone of Port Washington, N.Y. 6 cent stamp.
1970—Disabled American Veterans and American Prisoners of War Commemorative Issue. 6 cent stamp.

Airmail
1947—"Pan American Union Building" showing U.S. flag flying from atop the building. 10 cent stamp.
1959—"Balloon and Crowd" showing balloon aloft with two U.S. flags. 7 cent stamp.
1969—"First Man on the Moon" showing U.S. flag on suit of astronaut. 10 cent stamp.

The Flag on Postage Stamps

The American Flag on Foreign Stamps
1938—Ecuador. Issued to commemorate the 150th anniversary of the Constitution of the United States of America. Shows portrait of Washington and flags.
1958—Honduras. Issued to publicize the Honduras Institute of Inter-American Cultures. The proceeds were intended for the Bi-National Center, Tegucigalpa. Shows flags of Honduras and U.S. in original color.
1959—Honduras. Issued to commemorate the sesquicentennial of the birth of Abraham Lincoln. Shows Lincoln and Lincoln's birthplace backed by flags of both nations.
1959—Nicaragua. Shows Nicaraguan, Papal and United States flags.
1938—Panama. Shows Cathedral Tower and Statue of Liberty, flags of Panama and United States.
1950—Paraguay. Shows Franklin D. Roosevelt backed with Paraguayan and United States flags.
1959—El Salvador. Shows Presidents Eisenhower and Lemus and flags of both Nations.
1959—China. Shows President Sun Yat-sen and President Lincoln and flags of both nations.
1947—Philippines. Shows pictures of Presidents Manuel Quezon and Franklin D. Roosevelt, backed by the flags of both nations.
1947—San Marino. Shows portrait of President F. D. Roosevelt with flags of both nations. San Marino is the smallest and one of the oldest republics in Europe. Pope Urban VIII recognized San Marino as an independent State in 1631. It is located on a mountaintop in the Apennine Mountains of eastern Italy.
1939—Turkey. Shows Presidents Inonu and F. D. Roosevelt and Map of North America with Turkish and American flags.
1970—Uruguay. Shows Dwight D. Eisenhower with the background of the United States flag. In the margin of the stamp is "Medina—Imp. Nacional 1970."

When First Flown over a School

In June, 1903, the Catamount Hill Association of Colrain, Mass., set up a block of native stone on which these words were carved. "The first U.S. Flag Raised Over A Public School Was Floated In May, 1812 From A Log School-House Which Stood on This Spot." Mrs. Fanny Bowen Shippee, who took part in the flag raising, wrote this poem about the event:

> "Mrs. Rhoda Shippee, who stood for the right,
> Gave cloth for the stars and the field of pure white;
> It was wove on her loom, and hatchelled from tow,
> And of beautiful finish, as white as the snow.
> And Mrs. Lois Shippee for the "union" gave blue,
> Which she spun, colored, and wove—it was lovely to view;
> They made no long speeches, they made no long prayer,
> But of those who were gifted a plenty were there.
> There was no sounding of trumpet, no beating of drum,
> No tramping or marching, no firing of gun.
> But the farmers were there, attired in their frocks,
> And plenty of children, without slippers or socks.
> And they planted that staff, and worked with a will,
> 'Twas straight as an arrow, and as trim as a quill,
> And all the people were there from "the Hill."
> They stood there in groups a-waiting to see
> That emblem so grand—The Flag of the Free!"

In 1861 the Principal of the Fifth Street Grammar School in New Bedford, Mass. raised the flag over his small schoolhouse on May 11th.

In 1888, Youth's Companion, published in Boston,

When First Flown over a School

printed Francis Bellamy's "Pledge of Allegiance" which was repeated by more than 12 million school children at the 400th Anniversary of the Discovery of America by Columbus. President Harrison issued a proclamation that October 21, 1892 be declared a holiday, and that "the National Flag float over every schoolhouse in the country."

Flag Saluting in Schools

The first "flag salute" statute was passed in 1898 —on the day after the United States declared war on Spain—by the legislature of New York, and provided that...

"... *It shall be the duty of the state superintendent of public instruction to prepare, for the use of the public schools of the state, a program providing for a salute to the flag at the opening of each day of school, and such other patriotic exercises as may be deemed by him to be expedient, under such regulations and instructions as may best meet the varied needs of the different grades in such schools.*"

Rhode Island, Arizona, Kansas and Maryland all passed similar statutes.

After World War I, a different type of flag-salute law was passed in 1918.

Washington State legislature decreed:

"*Every board of directors ... shall cause appropriate flag exercises to be held in every school at least once in each week at which exercises the pupils shall recite the following salute to the flag:*—"*I pledge allegiance to my flag and the republic for which it stands, one nation indivisible, with liberty and justice for all.*"

If a teacher or school officer failed to carry out this provision they were dismissed.

Delaware, New Jersey and Massachusetts also passed such laws. As time went on, the laws became more stringent. The legislatures of these states felt that without the application of rewards and punishments, many teachers would not try to inculcate loyalty and patriotism in their students. In Massachusetts, teachers were made to take a special loyalty oath.

Patriotic organizations came to the support of the flag salute ceremony as a part of the school program in the United States, particularly after World War I.

The American Legion at their first convention

Flag Saluting in Schools

passed a resolution calling for state laws requiring that the flag be displayed at all public gatherings and during school hours over school buildings and that at least ten minutes per day be allotted to patriotic exercises in all public and private schools. By 1924 an estimated six and a half million leaflet copies of the 1923 Flag Code had been distributed free to school children.

The Veterans of Foreign Wars; the Daughters of the American Revolution and Children of that organization; The Sons of the American Revolution; and many other organizations took pride in seeing that the flag salute ceremony was in all schools.

By 1930 eighteen states had statutory provisions calling for some sort of teaching regarding the flag as well as saluting the flag.

The states worded their instructions differently but all insisted on flag respect, appropriate ceremonies, use, display, respect or etiquette. Several required their teachers to teach flag respect by precept and example. Some passed legislation to encourage school authorities to make some use of the flag salute ceremony.

Some states, such as New Jersey, Ohio and Pennsylvania, used the flag salute and ceremony in their schools long before those states had any supporting legislation.

The flag salute was used state-wide in nine states having flag-salute statutes and in most instances required flag instruction.

By 1940 it was in use in twenty four states: California, Colorado, Connecticut, Delaware, Florida, Georgia, Idaho, Kansas, Maryland, Massachusetts, Minnesota, Nebraska, New Hampshire, New Jersey, New York, Ohio, Oklahoma, Oregon, Pennsylvania, Texas, Vermont, Virginia, Washington and Wyoming.

Famous Large Flags

The original Star-Spangled Banner, measuring 30 × 42 feet, flew over Fort McHenry.

Civil War Veterans carried a mammoth flag up Pennsylvania Avenue during a reunion of the Grand Army of the Republic held in Washington, D.C., fifty years after the close of the Civil War. It was so heavy that 60 veterans had to carry it.

Mill-Workers in Manchester, New Hampshire, during World War I made a huge flag. It was four stories high. It weighed 200 pounds and was 50 × 95 feet in size. The stars were one yard in diameter, and were placed 4 feet 9 inches apart. The field of the union was 28 × 38 feet. Harlan A. Marshall took a picture of it affixed to the factory wall. It was surrounded by the employees who wove and made up the flag. It was written up by the National Geographic Society in their Flag Book published in 1917. The flag had 48 stars in the union.

Annin & Company made the world's largest free-flying flag, 60 × 90 feet, which is displayed on flag holidays from the New Jersey Towers of the George Washington Bridge, connecting New Jersey and New York. It weighs more than 500 pounds and has a link chain sewed into the heading by which it is hung.

Dettra Flag Company made a cotton bunting United States Flag measuring 66 × 96 feet, which was hung in The Convention Hall at Atlantic City, New Jersey. It covered the entire stage end of the auditorium.

J. L. Hudson Company, a department store in Detroit, claims the distinction of owning two of the largest flags in the world. It was on Armistice Day, November 11, 1923, that Hudson's original Largest

Famous Large Flags

Flag was unfurled for the first time. For 26 years it was the World's Largest Flag and was shown once a year. It measured 90 × 200 feet and was made by Annin & Co. Their second Largest Flag measures 104 × 235 feet and has been shown once a year since 1949.

The Largest Flag in the World

Unique, unusual and a sight to thrill Americans of all ages is the largest flag in the world, displayed with great pride by the J. L. Hudson Company of Detroit, Michigan. The flag they display today is much larger than the original which was unfurled for the first time on Armistice Day, November 11, 1923. Now it covers seven stories of Hudson's big Downtown store. Its long and eventful history includes its display on the U.S. Capitol in Washington, D.C. in 1929. To provide for proper care of the flag, Hudson's sent several representatives to Washington. Since no building was large enough to hold the banner, a scaffold nine stories high and 200 feet wide was built. The flag was also on exhibit at the New York World's Fair in 1939.

The second giant version of Old Glory made its debut on Flag Day, June 14, 1949. For six months the George P. Johnson Company of Detroit worked on the flag. Eight women worked at sewing machines for more than 700 hours. It took three sailmakers to put in the webbing, ropes and metal grommets for the ropes. In March, 1960, six women sewed a new field for the flag to include stars for the two new states, Alaska and Hawaii. It took them three weeks to complete their job and they added about 200 yards of white bed sheeting to the already gigantic flag.

America's Largest Old Glory is woven of finest grade shrinkproof army wool. It measures 235 feet long by 104 feet high. Each star is 6 feet tall, each stripe is 8 feet wide (requiring two specially woven 4 foot widths of wool). Materials include 2,038 yards of wool, 5,500 yards of thread, 57 yards of heavy canvas and more than a mile of strong rope to hold the flag to the building against the tug of the wind and its own weight. Altogether, the material is sufficient to make 611 flags, each 5 × 8 feet. It takes a crew of 55 men to handle this three-quarter ton flag, and its wooden packing case itself weighs 250 pounds.

Flag Makers

There are hundreds of flag makers in the U.S. ranging in size from small, one-man shops to large well-organized operations that turn out millions of flags a year.

Annin & Co. is the oldest flag maker in the country and one of the largest. In 1820, Alexander Annin, a ship chandler, began to supply ships in New York Harbor with U.S. flags. Before long his flag business began to outgrow the rest and in 1847 he established the firm as Annin & Co.

From that time on, Annin flags have been interwoven into the Nation's history. Beginning with the inauguration of Zachary Taylor, they have been at every inauguration since. They also include flags carried to the ends of the earth by Admiral Robert E. Peary on his North Pole expedition and by Admiral Richard E. Byrd on his expedition to the South Pole.

Fervid emotions are involved with the National Emblem and all flag makers are viewed as "custodians" of the flag. Thus, the company is a reliable source of information on flag etiquette and customs, and it directs as much effort at encouraging respect for the flag as at urging its display. Accordingly, Annin sponsors, and from time to time presents, the "Betsy Ross Award" to individuals who have furthered the cause of patriotism by some meritorious deed or contribution. Annin designed the 50-star flag and has 2,000 patterns of various sizes of the Stars and Stripes. Every year they make millions of flags, ranging in size from miniature flags 2×3 inches in size to exceptionally large sizes for social displays, such as the 60×90 foot free flying flag displayed at the George Washington Bridge which spans the Hudson River at New York City. To promote understanding and appreciation of the origins of our flag, they have created a special set of Historic Flags of Our Country which includes many of the flags illustrated on pp. 3, 4, and 5 of this book.

Flag Terms and Phrases

Badge: An emblem or other device displayed on a flag, generally in the hoist.

Banner: Originally a large medieval flag, rectangular in shape and usually carried in battle. Today the word is synonymous with flag.

Canton: The four quarters of a flag are named cantons, but this word is applied particularly to the upper canton in the hoist, that is, the upper left hand corner of the flag; the canton is sometimes also called the union.

Color: Specifically, a flag carried by an infantry or other dismounted military unit; more generally, any flag, as in the phrase, national colors.

Dipping: Practice, formerly followed, of merchant vessels lowering their ensigns in salute on meeting a naval vessel. The practice was also, on occasion, observed between warships.

Field: The surface of a flag on which the canton, badges, and other devices and designs are placed.

Fly: The portion of a flag farthest from the hoist.

Hoist: The portion of a flag nearest the flagstaff.

Jack: A flag, smaller than the ensign, flown at the bow by warships when at anchor or dressed with flags for a special event. Occasionally, it is also flown by other vessels.

Merchant Flag: A flag flown by a commercial or other private vessel; sometimes the same as the national flag, sometimes different from it.

National Color: A term designating the United States Flag carried by dismounted or unmounted units.

National Ensign: A term designating the United States Flag flown by airships, ships and boats.

National Flag: A flag representing a country; its use is sometimes restricted to the Government, but more often extended to the citizens in general. The term, when applied specifically to the United States Flag, refers to that flag in general without regard to a particular size or a manner of display.

Flag Terms and Phrases

National Standard: A term designating the United States Flag carried by mounted, mechanized and motorized units.

Pennant: A narrow flag which tapers gently toward the fly. Warships frequently fly masthead pennants.

Union: A design, signifying union, used on a national emblem. It is the honor point of the flag. On the United States Flag, it is the blue field containing the group of white stars.

To "hoist" or "raise a flag," is to draw the banner to the top of a pole, staff or mast, usually for the first time, as Washington did, at Cambridge, Massachusetts, January 1, 1776, and Lincoln raised a new flag over Independence Hall, Philadelphia, February 22, 1861.

To "dip the flag" is to lower it slightly then raise it quickly, as on shipboard, to salute another vessel or a fort.

The "flag at half-mast" means mourning. When a President, Governor, or other high official dies, flags are lowered half way, or "at half-mast," as a sign of mourning. Sometimes the memory of a private citizen, not an official, is honored in this way. Fishing craft and other vessels returning with flags at half-mast show that someone has been lost at sea.

To "strike the flag" is to lower it altogether as a sign of surrender or submission.

The Flag Research Center

The Flag Research Center, 17 Farmcrest Ave., Lexington, Mass. 02173, was established in 1962 to collect information on all kinds of flags and make this available to interested persons. It publishes books and charts on flags, as well as the quarterly FLAG BULLETIN. Flag information may be obtained by writing to the Director, Dr. Whitney Smith.

How Well Do You Know Old Glory?

Can you draw an accurate picture of the flag? Most of us could do a reasonable job, but how much of the following would be omitted from your drawing?

The flag has 13 horizontal stripes of equal width, seven red separated by six white.

The union or canton consists of 50 five-pointed white stars on a blue field, placed in the upper quarter next to the staff and extending to the lower edge of the fourth red stripe from the top.

The union has nine staggered rows of stars, with six stars in five rows and five stars in four alternating rows, each with point upward.

Every accurate replica of the flag has standard proportions based on the width, or "hoist."

Assuming the hoist (height of flag from top to bottom) equals 1, then the proportion of the fly (length of flag from staff to free end) should be 1.9, the hoist of union (which contains the stars) should be 7/13, the fly of union should be 0.76, the width of each strip 1/13, and the diameter of each star 0.0616. (Prescribed by President William Howard Taft, Oct. 28, 1912.)

To determine the right size flag for a flagpole, the length of the flag should be approximately equal to one-fourth of the height of the pole: for example, for a 40-foot pole the flag should be 6 × 10 feet.

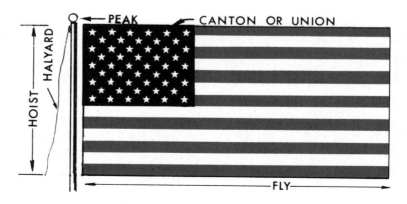

When the Flag Should Be Displayed

For nearly 150 years after Congress authorized the design for our flag, citizens had no uniform set of rules to guide them in displaying and showing respect for the flag.

To supply such a guide, a National Flag Conference was held in Washington, D.C. on Flag Day, June 14, 1923. Representatives of sixty-eight organizations met and drew up a Flag Code, which was revised by a second Conference in 1924.

Congress in 1942 adopted a resolution which made the Flag Code a law. This resolution was amended in December, 1942; and the Flag Code, as it is commonly called, became Public Law 829, 77th Congress.

Here are some of the provisions contained in it—

"It is the universal custom to display the flag from sunrise to sunset on buildings and on stationary flagstaffs that are in the open. However, the flag may be displayed at night out-of-doors upon special occasions when it is desired to produce a patriotic effect. The flag should be hoisted briskly and lowered ceremoniously. The flag should not be displayed out-of-doors on the days when the weather is inclement. The flag should be displayed daily, weather permitting, on or near the main administration building of every public institution. The flag should be displayed in or near every polling place on Election days. The flag should be displayed during school days in or near every school-house."

Special Days to Fly the Flag

Jan. 1. New Year's Day *
Jan. 20. Inauguration Day (Once every four years)
Jan. (3rd Mon.) Lee's Birthday (Ala. Miss. Va.)
Feb. (1st Mon.) Lincoln's Birthday (Ill. Del.)
Feb. 12. Lincoln's Birthday
Feb. (3rd Mon.) Washington's Birthday *
   President's Day (Haw.)
Easter Sun. (variable)
Mar. (1st Tues.) Town Meeting Day (Vt.)
Mar. 17. St. Patrick's Day
Mar. (Last Mon.) Seward's Day (Alaska)
Apr. (3rd Mon.) Patriot's Day (Maine, Mass.)
Apr. (4th Mon.) Confederate Memorial Day (Ala. Miss.)
Apr. (Last Fri.) Arbor Day (Utah)
May 1. Loyalty Day
May (2nd Sun.) Mother's Day
May (3rd Sat.) Armed Forces Day
May (Last Mon.) Memorial Day * (Half-staff until noon)
Jun. (1st Mon.) Jefferson Davis' Birthday (Ala. Miss.)
Jun. 14. Flag Day
Jun. (3rd Sun.) Father's Day
Jul. 4. Independence Day *
Aug. (2nd Mon.) Victory Day (R.I.)
Aug. (3rd Fri.) Admission Day (Haw.)
Sep. (1st Mon.) Labor Day *
Sep. 17. Citizenship Day, Constitution Day
Oct. (2nd Mon.) Columbus Day,* Farmer's Day (Fla.)
Oct. (3rd Mon.) Alaska Day (Alaska)
Oct. (4th Mon.) Veteran's Day *
Nov. (1st Tues.) Election Day
Nov. 11. Armistice Day (Miss.)
Nov. (Last Thurs.) Thanksgiving Day *
Dec. 21. Forefather's Day

Special Days to the Flag

Dec. 25. Christmas Day *

Denotes Federal Holiday

In addition, Birthdays of States and State Holidays, and such other days as may be proclaimed by the President.

National Flag Week

A Proclamation
By The President of The United States

On June 14, 1777, the Continental Congress meeting in Philadelphia adopted as a flag for the new nation a banner of 13 alternating red and white stripes and 13 white stars in a blue field. After nearly 200 years of history, only the constellation of stars in the flag has changed—from 13 to 50. The flag of the United States still symbolizes the dignity of man as it did when those early Americans created it. It evokes for us, besides, the memories of turbulent years and calm years, of men and women who have served its ideals in battle and in peace.

We honor the flag for what it is and for what it demands of us.

The Congress, by a joint resolution approved August 3, 1949 (63 Stat. 492), designated June 14 of each year as Flag Day and requested the President to issue annually a proclamation calling for its observance. The Congress, by a joint resolution approved June 9, 1966 (80 Stat. 194), also requested the President to issue annually a proclamation designating the week in which June 14 occurs as National Flag Week and calling upon all citizens to display the flag of the United States.

NOW, THEREFORE, I, RICHARD NIXON, President of the United States of America, do hereby designate the week beginning June 14, 1970, as National Flag Week, and I direct the appropriate government officials to display the flag of the United States on all government buildings during that week.

I also request the people to observe Flag Day, June 14, and Flag Week by flying the Stars and Stripes at their homes and other suitable places.

I urge the communications media to participate in and to promote this observance.

(Signed) **Richard Nixon**

Where the Flag Flies Day and Night

Four places where the flag flies day and night are in Maryland. The rest are scattered over the U.S.

(1) **Fort McHenry,** Baltimore, Maryland. By specific Legal Authority, granted in the joint Resolution of Congress described in Public Law 829.

Fort McHenry National Monument and Historic Shrine, ... Proclamation by President Harry S. Truman in July, 1948: "As a perpetual symbol of our patriotism, the Flag of the United States shall hereafter be displayed at Fort McHenry National Monument and Historical Shrine at all times during the day and night, except when the weather is inclement."

Throughout the courageous defense of this fort during the War of 1812 the national flag was never lowered. Thus it seemed particularly appropriate to authorize continued display of the Stars and Stripes, in peace as well as in war.

(2) **Flag House,** Flag House Square, Baltimore, Maryland, Public Law 319, approved March 26, 1954; "To permit the flying of the Flag of the United States for twenty-four hours of each day in Flag House Square." Also flown around the clock is a replica of the 15-starred, 15-striped flag of the War of 1812, famed as "The Star-Spangled Banner." The Flag House is the former home of Mary Young Pickersgill, who made the flag that Francis Scott Key saw flying over Fort McHenry early in the morning of September 14, 1814.

It was a very large flag, measuring 42 feet long and 30 feet wide. This flag, with eleven holes in it, made by the British bombshells, and with seven feet cut from it to wrap the body of one of the soldiers in the fort who died defending it, is now in the new Museum of History and Technology in Washington, D.C.

The original flag is backed by a new flag, showing the actual dimensions of the original.

Where the Flag Flies Day and Night

(3) **Mount Olivet Cemetery,** Frederick, Maryland. Here the national flag flies over the grave of Francis Scott Key, regardless of the weather.

(4) **Francis Scott Key Birthplace,** Keymar, Maryland, at Key's birthplace at Terra Rubra Farm, in Carroll County. It is marked by a stone monument. The Star-Spangled Banner has flown here day and night since May 30, 1949. The flag is maintained by the Kiwanis Club of Westminster, Maryland.

(5) **Marine Corps Memorial,** Arlington, Virginia. Proclamation by President John F. Kennedy on June 14, 1961: "Whereas the raising of the American Flag during that battle (Iwo Jima) over Mt. Suribachi, on February 23, 1945, symbolizes the courage and valor of the American fighting forces of World War II . . . proclaim that the Flag of the United States of America shall hereafter be displayed at the United States Marine Corps Memorial in Arlington, Virginia, at all times during the day and night except when the weather is inclement."

The memorial illustrates in statue form the photograph of this event made on Iwo Jima on March 26, 1945 by a Marine photographer, Joe Rosenthal. The statue was made by sculptor Felix de Weldon in 1954.

(6) **Worcester War Memorial,** Worcester, Massachusetts. The flag has been flying day and night at the Worcester War Memorial since 1933, honoring those who gave their lives in World War I.

(7) **United States Capitol,** Washington, D.C. A Congressional act of 1894 provided for the flying of the national flag over both the east and west fronts of the center of the Capitol. Flags fly over the Senate and House wings of the Capitol only when those legislative bodies are in session. (This was started in 1918.)

(8) **The Plaza,** Taos, New Mexico. The flag has flown longest at this place. In 1861, Kit Carson,

Where the Flag Flies Day and Night

assisted by Captain Smith H. Simpson of the United States Army, nailed a Union Flag to a pole in the Plaza at Taos as a symbol that citizens of New Mexico were loyal to the Union. During the Civil War their division of the Army saw to it that the flag flew there day and night. It has flown there ever since.

(9) The White House, Washington, D.C. President Richard M. Nixon, acting on the suggestion of the First Lady, Mrs. Patricia Nixon, issued a proclamation in September, 1970, directing that the flag be flown over the White House day and night.

* * *

The Star-Spangled Banner flies in several other places because of long-established custom or under the authority of the language of the Joint Resolution of December 22, 1942, which states that "The flag may be displayed at night upon special occasions when it is desired to produce a patriotic effect." The "special occasion" has, by practice in some places become "day and night." Such places are listed below:

    Little Bighorn Battlefield, Montana
    Mount Stover, Colton, California
    Pike's Peak, Colorado
    Deadwood, South Dakota

* * *

On June 11, 1967, The Star-Spangled Banner flew again over Fort McHenry, Baltimore, Maryland.

A replica of The Star-Spangled Banner, 30 × 42 feet, was hoisted at Fort McHenry by the United States Coast Guard Ceremonial Detail. This ceremony was sponsored by The Star-Spangled Banner Flag House Assn. Inc. It took 30 Coast Guardsmen to hold the flag so that it would not touch the ground while being hoisted over the fort.

Hats Off! The Flag is Passing By

In action, as well as in thought and word, we pay respect to the flag.

In THE FLAG GOES BY, Henry Holcomb Bennett describes the proper response to our flag in a passing parade. "Hats off! Along the street there comes a blare of bugles, a ruffle of drums, a flash of color beneath the sky . . ." The Flag Code tells us how the flag is properly displayed in a parade.

"The flag, when carried in a procession with another flag or flags should be either on the marching right; that is, the flag's own right, or if there is a line of other flags in front of the center of that line.

"The flag should not be displayed on a float in a parade except from a staff.

"The flag should not be draped over the hood, top, sides or back of a vehicle or of a railroad train or a boat. When the flag is displayed on a motorcar, the staff shall be fixed firmly to the chassis.

"When the flag is displayed otherwise than by being flown from a staff, it should be displayed flat, whether indoors or out, or so suspended that its folds fall as free as though the flag were staffed."

Our Flag Flies above All the Rest

Patriotic public-spirited citizens can look to the Flag Code for correct answers to questions regarding the display and use of the Flag of the United states.

The Flag Code, for example, gives the rules to follow when the Flag of the United States is displayed with the flag of the United Nations, or with other national or international flags.

The Flag Code, which was amended by an act of the 83rd Congress on July 9, 1953, reads as follows:

"No person shall display the flag of the United Nations or any other national or international flag equal, above, or in a position of superior prominence or honor to or in place of the Flag of the United States at any place within the United States or any Territory or possession thereof: Provided, that nothing in this section shall make unlawful the continuance of the practice heretofore followed of displaying the flag of the United Nations in a position of superior prominence or honor, and other national flags in positions of equal prominence or honor, with that of the Flag of the United States at the headquarters of the United Nations."

Respect when Flown with Other Flags

The Flag Code explains how our respect can best be shown on appropriate occasions when the Flag of the United States is displayed with one or more other flags or pennants.

"The Flag of the United States, when it is displayed with another flag against a wall from crossed staffs, should be on the right, the flag's own right; and its staff should be in front of the staff of the other flag.

"The Flag of the United States should be at the center and at the highest point of the group when a number of flags of States or localities or pennants of societies are grouped and displayed from staffs.

"When flags of States, cities, or localities, or pennants of societies are flown on the same halyard with the Flag of the United States, the latter should always be at the peak. When the flags are flown from adjacent staffs, the Flag of the United States should be hoisted first and lowered last. No such flag or pennant may be placed above the Flag of the United States or to the right of the Flag of the United States.

"When flags of two or more nations are displayed, they are to be flown from separate staffs of the same height. The flags should be of approximately equal size. International usage forbids the display of the flag of one nation above that of another nation in time of peace."

Unfurl Her Standards in the Air

These words are from THE AMERICAN FLAG, penned by Joseph Rodman Drake.

"Forever float that standard sheet! Where breathes the foe but falls before us, with Freedom's soil beneath our feet, and Freedom's banner streaming o'er us," he wrote about the flag.

Our flag, honored with these inspiring words as well as many others, should be properly displayed to reflect this honor. The Flag Code explains how this is accomplished.

"When the Flag of the United States is displayed from a staff projecting horizontally or at an angle from the window sill, balcony, or front of a building, the union of the flag (which contains the stars) should be placed at the peak of the staff unless the flag is at half-staff. When the flag is suspended over a sidewalk from a rope extending from a house to a pole at the sidewalk, the flag should be hoisted out, union first, from the building.

"When the flag is displayed over the middle of the street, it should be suspended vertically with the union to the north in an east and west street or to the east in a north and south street."

In Churches and Auditoriums

The Flag Code explains how the Flag of the United States is correctly placed in churches or on the speaker's platform in public auditoriums.

"When used on a speaker's platform, the flag, if displayed flat, should be displayed above and behind the speaker. When displayed from a staff in a church or public auditorium, if it is displayed in the chancel of a church, or on the speaker's platform in a public auditorium, the flag should occupy the position of honor and be placed at the clergyman's or speaker's right as he faces the congregation or audience. Any other flag so displayed in the chancel or on the platform should be placed at the clergyman's or speaker's left as he faces the congregation or audience.

"But when the flag is displayed from a staff in a church or public auditorium elsewhere than in the chancel or on the platform, it shall be placed in the position of honor at the right of the congregation or audience as they face the chancel or platform. Any other flag so displayed should be placed on the left of the congregation or audience as they face the chancel or platform."

During Public Affairs

Public affairs, parades, and gatherings provide opportunities for citizens to honor the flag.

This honor can be in song, in word or in deed, or all three, by means of our National Anthem, the Pledge of Allegiance, or action as explained in the Flag Code:

"During the ceremony of hoisting or lowering the flag or when the flag is passing in a parade or in a review, all persons present should face the flag, stand at attention, and salute. Those present in uniform should render the military salute. When not in uniform, men should remove the headdress with the right hand holding it at the left shoulder, the hand being over the heart. Men without hats should salute in the same manner. Aliens should stand at attention. Women should salute by placing the right hand over the heart. The salute to the flag in the moving column should be rendered at the moment the flag passes.

"When the National Anthem is played and the flag is not displayed, all present should stand and face toward the music. Those in uniform should salute at the first note of the anthem, retaining this position until the last note. All others should stand at attention, men removing the headdress. When the flag is displayed, all present face the flag and salute.

"The Pledge of Allegiance is rendered by standing with the right hand over the heart. However, civilians will always show full respect to the flag when the pledge is given by merely standing at attention, men removing the headdress. Persons in uniform shall render the military salute."

At Unveilings and Burial Services

On certain occasions, our flag is not only itself an object of respect; it is also a symbol of respect for something or someone else: Provisions for display:

"The flag should form a distinctive feature of the ceremony of unveiling a statue or monument, but it should never be used as the covering for the statue or monument.

"The flag, when flown at half-staff, should be first hoisted to the peak for an instant and then lowered to the half-staff position. The flag should be again raised to the peak before it is lowered for the day. By "half-staff" is meant lowering the flag to one-half the distance between the top and bottom of the staff. Crepe streamers may be affixed to spearheads or flagstaffs in a parade only by order of the President of the United States.

"When the flag is used to cover a casket, it should be so placed that the union is at the head and over the left shoulder. The flag should not be lowered into the grave or allowed to touch the ground."

The flag for the burial service of an honorably discharged veteran is furnished by the Veterans Administration, Washington, D.C. It may be obtained from the nearest post office upon presentation of proper proof of honorable discharge. The flag must be presented to the next of kin at the appropriate moment in the burial service. Should there be no relative present, or one cannot be located, the flag must be returned to the Veterans Administration.

Proper Respect for Our Flag

The flag should always be displayed in a proper and dignified manner.

There are precautions which should be followed to make sure that no disrespect is shown to our flag. These are in the Flag Code:

"No disrespect should be shown to the Flag of the United States; the flag should not be dipped to any person or thing. Regimental colors, State flags, and organization or institutional flags are to be dipped as a mark of honor.

"The flag should never be displayed with the union down save as a signal of dire distress.

"The flag should never touch anything beneath it, such as the ground, the floor, water or merchandise.

"The flag should never be carried flat or horizontally, but always aloft and free.

"The flag should never be used as drapery of any sort whatsoever, never festooned, drawn back, nor up, in folds, but always allowed to fall free. Bunting of blue, white and red, always arranged with the blue above, the white in the middle, and the red below, should be used for covering a speaker's desk, draping the front of a platform, and for decoration in general.

"The flag should never be fastened, displayed, used or stored in such a manner as will permit it to be easily torn, soiled, or damaged in any way."

How to Fold—Fold width-wise twice, leaving union exposed. Begin at striped end, fold into triangles. Repeat until only end of union is exposed. Tuck remaining end inside.

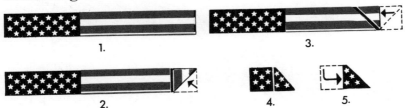

Our Flag Is Not a Decoration

The bold red, white and blue combination of colors in the Flag of the United States and the distinctive design command immediate attention of all who see them. This attention-arresting quality of our flag, however, should never be utilized for purely decorative purposes.

The Flag Code explains how mis-use and mistreatment of our flag can be avoided:

"The flag should never be used as a covering for a ceiling.

"The flag should never have placed upon it, nor on any part of it, nor attached to it any mark, insignia, letter, word, figure, design, picture, or drawing of any nature.

"The flag should never be used as a receptacle for receiving, holding, carrying, or delivering anything.

"The flag should never be used for advertising purposes in any manner whatsoever. It should not be embroidered on such articles as cushions or handkerchiefs and the like, printed or otherwise impressed on paper napkins or boxes or anything that is designed for temporary use and discard; or used as any portion of a costume or athletic uniform. Advertising signs should not be fastened to a staff or halyard from which the flag is flown.

"The flag, when it is in such condition that it is no longer a fitting emblem for display, should be destroyed in a dignified way, preferably by burning."

The only agency allowed by law to use the Flag in an advertisement is the United States Government.

When Flown at Half-Staff

Apparently, no definite instructions for flying the flag at half-staff were established in the early years of our country's history. As a result, many conflicting regulations existed.

In 1954, President Eisenhower issued instructions stating when, and for what length of time, the Flag of the United States should fly at half-staff:

"For thirty days from the day of death of the President or a former President.

"For ten days in the case of the death of the Vice President, the Chief Justice or a retired Chief Justice, or the Speaker of the House of Representatives.

"From the day of death until interment for an Associate Justice of the Supreme Court, a member of the Cabinet, a former Vice President, the Secretaries of the Army, Navy and Air Force, a United States Senator, a member of the House, a territorial delegate, the Resident Commissioner of the Commonwealth of Puerto Rico, or the Governor of a state or territory."

"In the event of the death of other officials, former officials or foreign dignitaries, the flag should be displayed at half-staff, in accordance with such orders or instructions as might be issued by or at the direction of the President, or in accordance with recognized customs or practices not inconsistent with law."

The President's proclamation also stated that "the heads of departments and agencies of the Federal Government might direct that the flag be flown at half-staff on occasions other than those specified which they consider proper.

On March 29, 1969, President Nixon ordered all flags flown at half-staff for mourning for Gen. Eisenhower for 30 days.

Misuse of the Flag

Down through our history there have been people in the United States who, for one reason or another, have desecrated the flag to show contempt for the United States.

As early as 1800 a man in New Orleans was convicted by a military commission and hanged for tearing down a United States flag that flew over the Mint.

In the late 1800's, use of our flag to advertise products shocked many people. They resented the exploitation of our flag which appeared on whiskey bottles, tin cans and on sides of barns advertising everything from cough syrup to chewing tobacco.

A flag misuse bill was drafted in 1880 but never got to the Congress.

In 1897, patriotic societies founded the American Flag Association and declared war on exploiters of the flag.

During the Presidential compaign of 1896 between William McKinley and William Jennings Bryan, the then-President of the now defunct American Flag Association said:

"That year the Presidential tickets were fastened to the flag... I condemn not the spirit of 1896, which led to the use of the flag that year so freely for political purposes, but I condemn the use."

Because of the stand this organization took, many states enacted flag-desecration statutes, specifically banning advertisements showing the flag.

Today, every state has a law forbidding defacing, desecration, or showing disrespect for the flag of the United States. They provide penalties ranging from a $5 to $10 fine in Indiana, to a maximum sentence of 25 years imprisonment in Texas.

In 1968 Congress passed an act setting penalties for casting contempt on the flag. The Federal law declared that a person may be imprisoned for up to a year and/or fined up to $1,000 for intentionally

Misuse of the Flag

casting contempt upon the United States Flag, a piece of one or a picture of one, or "publicly mutilating, defacing, defiling, burning or trampling on it."

Patriotic organizations in every state are cracking down on people who desecrate the flag. One enterprising manufacturer of ladies undergarments tried recently to market a girdle overprinted with the stars and stripes. The Daughters of the American Revolution heard about it and attacked in force and the girdles were withdrawn from sale. And an American tennis player who appeared in England with a flag imprinted on her shorts was severely criticized.

In addition, old state laws have been hauled off the shelves to prosecute people for burning flags, washing a flag in public, flying a flag upside down, wearing clothes patched with flags, displaying flags with peace symbols or slogans on them, or for failure to salute the flag.

Use of New and Superseded Flags

The White House, on August 21, 1959, issued the following statement governing the use of the then new 50 star flag and the 49 and 48 star flags which it superseded.

"By law, the new 50 star flag will become the official flag of the United States on July 4, 1960, the birthday of the Union. Display of the new flag before that time will be improper. However it is not improper to display the 48 star flag or the 49 star flag after that date; with limited exceptions agencies of the Federal Government will continue to display the 48 star flag and the 49 star flag so long as they remain in good condition and until existing stocks of unused flags are exhausted. It is appropriate for all citizens to do the same."

Opinion of the U.S. Supreme Court

by Justice John Marshall Harlan

In a court case, Halter and Haywood v. State of Nebraska, 205 U.S. 34, Justice John Marshall Harlan of the Supreme Court of the United States gave this opinion, on March 4, 1907. (Desecration of the Flag)

"From the earliest periods in the history of the human race, banners, standards and ensigns have been adopted as symbols of the power and history of the peoples who bore them. It is not then remarkable that the American people, acting through legislative branch of the Government, early in their history, prescribed a flag as symbolic of the existence and sovereignty of the Nation. Indeed, it would have been extraordinary if the Government had started this country upon its marvelous career without giving it a flag to be recognized as the emblem of the American Republic. No American, nor any foreign born person who enjoys the privileges of American citizenship, ever looks upon it without taking pride in the fact that he lives under this free Government. Hence, it has often occurred that insults to a flag in the presence of those who revere it, have been resented and, sometimes, punished on the spot . . . So, a State may exert its power to strengthen the bonds of the Union and patriotism and love of Country among its people. When, by its legislation, the State encourages a feeling of patriotism towards a Nation, it necessarily encourages a like feeling towards the State. One who loves the Union will love the State in which he resides, and love, both of the common country and of the state will diminish in proportion as respect for the flag is weakened. Therefore, a State will be wanting in care for the well-being of its people if it ignores the fact that they regard the flag as a symbol of their Country's power and prestige, and will be impatient if any open disrespect is shown towards it. To every

Opinion of the United States Supreme Court

true American the flag is the symbol of the Nation's power, the emblem of freedom in its truest, best sense.

"*It is not extravagant to say that to all lovers of the Country it signifies government resting on the consent of the governed; liberty regulated by law; the protection of the weak against the strong; security against the exercise of arbitrary power; and absolute safety for free institutions against foreign aggression. As the statute in question evidently had its origin in a purpose to cultivate a feeling of patriotism among the people of the State, we are unwilling to adjudge that, in legislation for that purpose, the State erred in duty or has infringed the constitutional right of anyone. On the contrary, it may reasonably be affirmed that a duty rests upon each State in every legal way to encourage its people to love the Union with which the State is indissolubly connected.*

"*Displaying the National Flag to the exclusion of the State flag, except on purely state occasions, has now extended to practically all States. Each State when they came into the Union, assumed certain obligations respecting the symbol of the Union, the United States Flag, and enacted adequate laws for the protection of the United States Flag and to provide penalties for its desecration.*"

John Marshall Harlan (1833–1911) was Associate Justice of the United States Supreme Court for almost thirty-four years. He was known as "the GREAT DISSENTER" because of his strongly individual interpretation of the law.

He defended civil liberties and the rights of Negroes given them by the amendments to the Constitution passed after the War between the States.

This was the first case brought to the Supreme Court of the U.S. for desecration of the flag. Halter and Haywood were two beer salesman who sold beer in bottles picturing the flag of the U.S.

Bibliography

Aikman, Lonnelle, **"New Stars for Old Glory,"** National Geographic Magazine, July, 1959, pages 86–121

Allegheny Trails Council, **Broad Stripes and Bright Stars** (American Heritage, 1970)

Barraclough, E. M. C., **Flags of the World** (Warne, 1969)

Blassingame, Wyatt, **The Story of the United States Flag** (Garrard, 1969)

Calvert, James, **"I Pledge Allegiance,"** Whittlesey, 1952

Capron, Walter C., Captain, **U.S. Coast Guard,** New York, Franklin Watts, Inc., 1965

Carmer, Carl Lamson, **A Flag for the Fort,** Jr. Literary Guild, 1961

Eggenberger, David, **Flags of the U.S.A.,** Crowell, 1964

Elting, Mary and Franklin Folsom, **Flags of All Nations and the People Who Live Under Them** (Grosset & Dunlap, 1969)

Freeman, Mae Blacker, **Stars and Stripes,** Random House, 1964

Glick, Carl, **The Story of Our Flag,** New York, Putnam, 1964

Greene, Daniel, **"What Is It We Rally 'Round?"** The National Observer, July 13, 1970

"Who Owns the Stars and Stripes?" Time, July 6, 1970

Harrison, Peleg Dennis, **The Stars and Stripes,** Boston, Little Brown & Co. 1914

Kerrick, Harrison Summers, **The Flag of the United States,** The Champlin Printing Co., 1925

Krythe, Maymie R., **What So Proudly We Hail,** N.Y., Harper and Row, 1968

Lee, Tina Dorothy, **Flag Day,** Crowell, N.Y., 1965

Manwaring, David Roger, **Render Unto Caesar,** Chicago, Univ. of Chicago Press, 1962

Bibliography

McCandless, Byron, **Flags of the World,** National Geographic Society, Wash., D.C. 1917

McSpadden, Joseph Walker, **Flag Day,** Crowell, 1940

Mendenhall, Thomas Corwin, **A Flag Episode,** Worcester, Mass. 1899

Miller, Margarette S., **I Pledge Allegiance,** Boston, The Christopher Pub. House 1946

Miller, Natalie, **The Story of the Star-Spangled Banner,** Chicago, Children's Press, 1965

National Geographic Society, **Great Adventures with National Geographic,** Washington, D.C. 1963

Navy, Magazine of Sea Power, March, 1965

Preble, George Henry, **Our Flag,** Albany, J. Munsell, 1872

Quaife, Milo Milton, **The Flag of the U.S.,** New York, Grosset & Dunlap, 1942

Quaife, Milo; Weig, Melvin; Appleman, Roy: **The History of the United States Flag,** Phila., Eastern Nat. Park and Monument Assn. 1961 (later work)

Review, Pub. Defense Supply Assn. Sept., 1968, United States Coast Guard, by H. R. Kaplan

Rivers, A. M., **History of the American Flag** (Vantage, 1967)

Sigmon, Mrs. Martin L., **The Flag of the U.S.,** National Society of the D.A.R., 1936

Smith, Whitney, **The Flag Book of the United States** (Morrow, 1970)

Washburn, Harold Connett, 1884, Illustrated Case inscriptions from the official catalogue of the Flags of the U.S. Navy. The Lord Baltimore Press, 1913

Werstein, Irving, **The Stars and Stripes: The Story of Our Flag** (Golden Press, 1969)

Winslow, Ola Elizabeth, selected and edited by: **American Broadside Verse,** Yale University Press, New Haven, Conn. 1930